OXFORD STUDENT TEXTS

Series Editor: Steven Croft

Shakespeare's Sonnets

D1007750

Shakespeare's Sonnets

Edited by Deborah West

Oxford University Press

OXFORD
UNIVERSITY PRESS

Great Clarendon Street, Oxford OX2 6DP

Oxford University Press is a department of the University of Oxford.
It furthers the University's objective of excellence in research, scholarship,
and education by publishing worldwide in

Oxford   New York

Auckland   Cape Town   Dar es Salaam   Hong Kong   Karachi
Kuala Lumpur   Madrid   Melbourne   Mexico City   Nairobi
New Delhi   Shanghai   Taipei   Toronto

With offices in

Argentina   Austria   Brazil   Chile   Czech Republic   France   Greece
Guatemala   Hungary   Italy   Japan   South Korea   Poland   Portugal
Singapore   Switzerland   Thailand   Turkey   Ukraine   Vietnam

Oxford is a registered trade mark of Oxford University Press
in the UK and in certain other countries

British Library Cataloguing in Publication Data
Data available

ISBN: 978-0-19-832576-5

1 3 5 7 9 10 8 6 4 2

Typeset in Goudy Old Style MT
by Palimpsest Book Production Limited, Grangemouth, Stirlingshire

Printed in Great Britain by Cox and Wyman Ltd., Reading

The Publishers would like to thank the following for permission to reproduce photographs:

p5: Bettmann/Corbis; p6: Oxford University Press; p10: Oxford University Press; p18: Oxford
University Press; p213: The Bridgeman Art Library; p214: National Portrait Gallery.

Artwork is by Martin Cottam.

Contents

Acknowledgements

The text of the sonnets is taken with permission from *The Complete Sonnets and Poems*, edited by Colin Burrow, Oxford World's Classics, 2002.

Lines from 'Sonnet 157' by Francesco Petrarch are reprinted from *Petrarch's Lyric Poems: The Rime sparse and other lyrics*, translated and edited by Robert M. Durling (Harvard University Press, 1976), copyright © Robert M. Durling 1976, by permission of the publisher.

Deborah West dedicates this book to Bryan. Thank you for being there.

Editors

Steven Croft, the series editor, holds degrees from Leeds and Sheffield universities. He has taught at secondary and tertiary level and is currently Head of the Department of English and Humanities in a tertiary college. He has 25 years' examining experience at A level and is currently a Principal Examiner for English. He has written several books on teaching English at A level and his publications for Oxford University Press include *Literature, Criticism and Style*, *Success in AQA Language and Literature* and *Exploring Language and Literature*.

Deborah West has degrees from both Sheffield University and The Shakespeare Institute, Stratford-upon-Avon, having reached doctoral standard. She has taught in further and higher education, and is currently Co-ordinator of English Literature in a tertiary college. She has worked as an A-level examiner for several years, and is a Senior Examiner for English. Her publications include *John Keats: Selected Poems* in the *Oxford Student Text* series and several A-level texts for the National Extension College.

Foreword

Oxford Student Texts, under the founding editorship of Victor Lee, have established a reputation for presenting literary texts to students in both a scholarly and an accessible way. The new editions aim to build on this successful approach. They have been written to help students, particularly those studying English literature for AS or A level, to develop an increased understanding of their texts. Each volume in the series, which covers a selection of key poetry and drama texts, consists of four main sections which link together to provide an integrated approach to the study of the text.

The first part provides important background information about the writer, his or her times and the factors that played an important part in shaping the work. This discussion sets the work in context and explores some key contextual factors.

This section is followed by the poetry or play itself. The text is presented without accompanying notes so that students can engage with it on their own terms without the influence of secondary ideas. To encourage this approach, the Notes are placed in the third section, immediately following the text. The Notes provide explanations of particular words, phrases, images, allusions and so forth, to help students gain a full understanding of the text. They also raise questions or highlight particular issues or ideas, which are important to consider when arriving at interpretations.

The fourth section, Interpretations, goes on to discuss a range of issues in more detail. This involves an examination of the influence of contextual factors as well as looking at such aspects as language and style, and various critical views or interpretations. A range of activities for students to carry out, together with discussions as to how these might be approached, are integrated into this section.

At the end of each volume there is a selection of Essay Questions, a Further Reading list and, where appropriate, a Glossary.

We hope you enjoy reading this text and working with these supporting materials, and wish you every success in your studies.

Steven Croft *Series Editor*

William Shakespeare in Context

The life of William Shakespeare

William Shakespeare was baptized in Holy Trinity Church, Stratford-upon-Avon, on 26 April 1564, probably having been born a couple of days before. His father, John, was a glover and chamberlain of the town, to become an even more important bailiff and justice of the peace in 1568. William's mother was Mary Arden, who came from a more prosperous family from neighbouring Wilmcote. John and Mary, having married in about 1552, bore many children: William was the eldest living child (1564–1616), with Gilbert (1566–1612), Joan (1569), Richard (1574) and Edmund (1580–1607) to follow.

It is likely that Shakespeare was educated at what is now King Edward IV Grammar School, where his staple academic diet would probably have been Latin, grammar, rhetoric, logic and the well-known literary works of the time. The days would have been long, beginning at around six or seven in the morning, and continuing until five or six; only Sundays were free from such academic rigour, and there were no long holidays to serve as respite. Shakespeare would have had a solid grounding in Protestantism, as the law and his father's role in the town would have required of him to visit church on Sundays and Holy Days. His schooling would have incorporated worship at Matins and Evensong, taking all forms of devotion from Queen Elizabeth I's Book of Common Prayer.

We do not know at what age Shakespeare left school, but his father's mounting debts may well have meant that he had to leave early. Perhaps he worked in the family business, or there is the possibility that he was sent to work elsewhere in order to bring money home. While this part of his history is murky, what we know for certain is that, in 1582, a 'William Shagspere' was given a licence to marry Anne Hathaway of Shottery. Coming from substantial yeoman stock, Anne brought with her a sizeable inheritance potential, in the form of a 12-room farmhouse. It is, today, known as Anne Hathaway's Cottage, but this name does not do justice to its value or magnitude. It is clear, from this one piece of architectural evidence, that Shakespeare's new bride was an heiress to a substantial fortune.

Shakespeare's marriage has fuelled endless speculation, not least because Anne Hathaway was seven years older than the 18-year-old William. She was also pregnant on her wedding day. On Sunday 26 May 1583, the newly married pair baptized Susanna. By 1585, the twins Hamnet and Judith had been born, completing the Shakespeare family.

The next seven years are a blank and have become known as 'the lost years'. Academics have attempted to fill in the gaps, but with little evidence and a great deal of romantic fabrication. The facts show that, at some point, William Shakespeare went to London and joined an acting company there. Perhaps he had caught the theatre bug from travelling acting troupes in Stratford, and more colourful myths suggest that he may have travelled with such a company nationwide before finally following them to London.

Early critics help us to date Shakespeare's dramatic work. Robert Greene wrote of him as an 'upstart crow' in 1592, implying that Shakespeare was already an established playwright in London by then. By referring to a line from *3 Henry VI*, Greene helps us to date this early play and the preceding ones in the trilogy. In 1598, Francis Meres, in his *Palladis Tamia: Wit's Treasury*, praised Shakespeare for his plays staged thus far:

> As Plautus and Seneca are accorded the best for comedy and tragedy among the Latins, so Shakespeare among the English is the most excellent in both kinds on the stage; for comedy, witness his *Gentle-men of Verona*, his *Errors*, his *Love Labour's Lost*, his *Love Labour's Won*, his *Midsummer's Night Dream* and his *Merchant of Venice*: for tragedy, his *Richard II*, *Richard III*, *Henry IV*, *King John*, *Titus Andronicus* and his *Romeo and Juliet*.

All of this dramatic output, added to the three parts of the *Henry* plays and *The Taming of the Shrew*, presents a staggering total of material for a 34-year-old writer.

We know that Shakespeare belonged to the Lord Chamberlain's Men, a London acting company later to become the King's Men during the reign of James I. It is probable that Shakespeare turned to his poetic writing during periods of plague in London, when the theatres were closed by law and all theatre workers were in need of extra income. It was seldom that a playwright published a playscript, as any rival acting company could then use the material; but poetry was different, and Shakespeare was to publish much verse during his lifetime.

Despite a long and successful working life in the capital, Shakespeare never bought a property in London, only ever lodging there; this perhaps suggests that he always considered Stratford to be his home. Again, there is not the evidence to inform us of how often he would have returned to his family, but we do know that such a journey would have been lengthy and arduous. Shakespeare must have resided, for the bulk of his time, in London, sending money home to his family and corresponding with them by letter. It is likely that Shakespeare sent regular money to his father, who was in debt until his death. Nonetheless, John Shakespeare was awarded the status of gentleman in 1596, after William applied for a family coat-of-arms in his name.

Tragically, William's son, Hamnet, also died in this same year, aged 11, an event that presumably brought his father back to Stratford. In the following year, Shakespeare procured for his family a very large house there, called New Place, a substantial dwelling that William would eventually retire to. It is difficult to state with any certainty when Shakespeare wrote his last play, but by 1613 it seems that he had left London in order to enjoy retirement in his native Stratford. He died on 23 April 1616, and the town register documents the burial of one 'Will Shakspere, gent.' two days later.

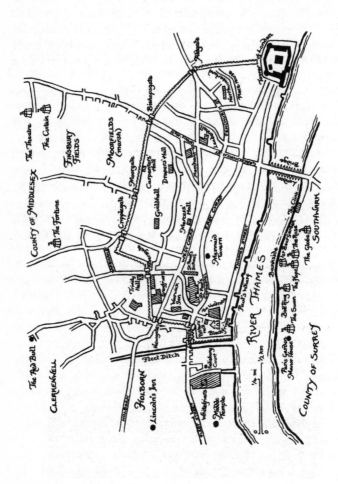

London theatres around 1600

Early Modern literature

The Early Modern period dated from around 1450 to the mid-seventeenth century. It encapsulated the beginning of standard forms of the English language, as well as Early Modern tendencies, characteristics and thoughts, all of which helped to shape the arts. Early Modern England saw new and exciting forms of painting, architecture, sculpture and poetry.

We know that it was the newly established theatres that drew Shakespeare to London. There had never been anything like them before; in the medieval period, all plays had been religious in nature and acted on carts that travelled the nation. It was a hard life for the players since scenery, costumes and all of life's essentials had also to be taken with them; and income was usually low, as they tended to perform in market squares or Inns of Court, where few spectators could gather. The new London playhouses were like nothing ever seen before: they performed full-length secular plays, based upon Greek and Roman legend and English

The view looking west up the River Thames, showing the Globe Theatre and the Bear Garden; a detail from a panoramic view of London by Wenceslaus Hollar, c. 1670.

history, and used the blank verse that the Earl of Surrey had introduced earlier in the sixteenth century. The first playhouse, The Theatre, was built in 1576 by James Burbage in Shoreditch just outside the City's boundary.

By the time that Shakespeare went to London, many more playhouses had been built and were firmly established as a part of City life. The Globe Theatre was built in 1599, in Southwark, housing up to 3,000 spectators. This theatre, like all the others, acted as a way of distributing much of the social, political and religious output of the day; and, despite censorship, ideas seemed to be generated quite freely.

Shakespeare's company, the Lord Chamberlain's Men (to become the King's Men in May 1603), had worked in several playhouses before the Globe Theatre was built. Shakespeare was one of eight people to pool his finances and skills in order to get the Globe project off the ground. As a result, Shakespeare co-owned, planned, wrote and even acted for his new enterprise; and,

The Swan Theatre copied by Arend van Buchell from an original sketch by Dutch student, Johannes de Witt, 1596

as Andrew Gurr writes, '[his acting company] ran unbroken for forty-eight years. No other company lasted more than ten, and most enjoyed no more than three in London' (1987, p. 70).

One of the most popular playwrights of the day was Christopher Marlowe (1564–93), whose career came to a rather abrupt end when he was killed in a Deptford tavern. His *Tamburlaine the Great*, along with Thomas Kyd's (1558–95) *The Spanish Tragedy*, Ben Jonson's (1572–1637) *The Alchemist* and John Webster's (d. 1634) *The White Devil* were dramatic compositions that had never been witnessed before, and the playwrights were the great wits with whom Shakespeare was in competition.

But Shakespeare was not just a successful playwright; we know that he wrote much poetry too – epics, as well as his shorter lyric poems. Indeed, the Golden Age of literature was announced with much magnificent poetry and prose, created by those who were to herald the dawn of the new age. Shakespeare would have read the works of Edmund Spenser (1552–99), for example, who had produced his pastoral poem *The Shepherds' Calendar* (1579), while Sir Philip Sidney (1554–86) had outlined the theories of poetry in his *The Apology for Poetry* (c. 1580) and published his prose romance, *Arcadia* (1590). Edmund Spenser's *The Faerie Queene* began to be published from 1590, a few books at a time, and those that were to become known as the Metaphysical poets were leaving their mark with a new brand of wit.

Early Modern London

Early Modern London was an important city, in that it was the capital of England, the seat of royal and political power, a major port on the River Thames, the centre for finance and a major cultural quarter. In the Early Modern period, the city itself, as well as its extensive suburbs, drew in many nationals and Europeans, extending its perimeters and its powers.

Early Modern Europe was what can be termed nationalistic. Each nation state had its own language, cultural ideologies, policies, religious beliefs and sense of morality. Each vied for supremacy, and England was no exception. The royal court assumed the position of centre of power and it was here that patronage – political sponsorship and protection – was given, and a man's future was made or destroyed.

Such English nationalism was further strengthened by religious policy. Henry VIII's (1491–1547) break with Rome, and the dissolution of the monasteries, meant that Protestantism ruled supreme. Henry's daughter, Elizabeth, was seen to take on the same role as Defender of the Faith and Supreme Head of the Church. Essentially, England was answerable to no one.

Nonetheless, during the period that Shakespeare worked in London, Elizabethan city life was hard. The poor harvests of the 1590s, along with the wars with Spain, depleted the economy and left Londoners wanting. The poor and the desperate were fast outgrowing those employed to control them and unease was spreading as an ageing queen, with no heir to succeed her, left rumours circulating that James VI of Scotland would become England's next monarch as James I.

Despite such concerns, the accession of the new king, James I, brought a wealth of rejoicing to mark his procession from Edinburgh to London. He was crowned on 31 March 1603 and the country's feeling of security and peace was matched with a revival of trade and the influx of many visitors from Europe, hoping for preferment.

The plague

Such hope was short-lived, however, as the increased activity meant the return of the plague and by May of 1603, it had destroyed many aspects of Elizabethan and Jacobean life, resulting in many years of great depression. As well as killing and maiming in its thousands, it also put paid to both domestic and export trade, and the transaction of even local business.

The playhouses were also told to close when plague struck, which pleased the Privy Council since actors had always been considered vagabonds and their premises dens of iniquity. All acting companies were then forced either to live on money made thus far or to become travelling players once again. It is known that Shakespeare attached himself to the various London acting companies that would employ him for his acting and playwriting skills, but it is difficult to state with any certainty whether he went with any one of them on their tours.

Twice during Shakespeare's working life, long and severe plague epidemics kept the playhouses closed. From June 1592 to June 1594, they were hardly ever open and between March 1603 and April 1604 constant interruptions meant that it was hardly worth opening the Globe Theatre. Further outbreaks of the plague, from 1605 to 1609, meant that there were some disruptions, but the closures were very spaced out helping the companies to gain respite in between.

The shutdown of 1592 came at a point in Shakespeare's career when he was just beginning to make a name for himself. Rather than be idle during this period of interruption, it is safe to say that he turned at least some of his attention to the composition of poetry. His two long narrative poems were written while the playhouses were shut and their success gave him the literary reputation that the more popular consumption of playwriting never could. *Venus and Adonis* was printed in 1593, an Ovidian mock epic given an erotic twist by Shakespeare; it ran through an impressive 11 editions in 27 years. *The Rape of Lucrece* was printed in 1594; based on the *Chronicles*, it stood as a historical tragedy.

The sonnet sequence

The complete 154 sonnet sequence was not printed until 1609 (another period of plague and theatrical cessation), although by this stage in his career, Shakespeare had become hugely successful, not because of his poetry, but because of his

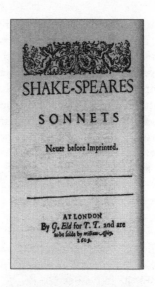

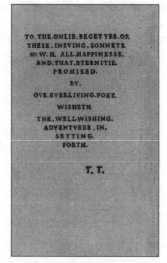

The title and dedication pages of the 1609 quarto edition of
Shakespeare's sonnets

dramatic work with the King's Men. It is clear that the sonnets had been written much before their publication date for, in 1598, Francis Meres had written of the circulation of the 'sugared sonnets among his private friends', suggesting that Shakespeare had attempted to improve his reputation in advance of print by allowing influential people to read and critique his material. In addition, in 1599, William Jaggard published *The Passionate Pilgrim*, which included two corrupt versions of Shakespeare's sonnets. By 1609, the publisher of what we now know as the quarto edition of the sonnets, Thomas Thorpe, produced rather an ambiguous title page saying 'Never before imprinted'.

Shakespeare's dedication and the youth

Although we know that Shakespeare sold his sonnets, there is no evidence that he had any hand in their publication. The dedication by the publisher, Thomas Thorpe, in 1609 has proved to add still more enigmatic questions to the mystery:

> To the only begetter of these ensuing sonnets Mr W.H. all happiness and that eternity promised by our ever-living poet wisheth the well-wishing adventurer in setting forth.   T.T.

The question of who Mr W.H. – 'the only begetter' – actually was has never been satisfactorily answered. Over the years, there have been many tenuous attempts to both identify W.H. in isolation and to cast him as the real persona behind the poet's young male friend.

The two most quoted models for Mr W.H.'s – and, thereby, the youth's – identity are Henry Wriothesley (the W.H. initials in reverse), the Earl of Southampton and William Herbert, the Earl of Pembroke.

Each of these men knew and served as patrons to Shakespeare. Both *Venus and Adonis* and *The Rape of Lucrece* had been dedicated to the Earl of Southampton and the posthumously published collection of Shakespeare's work, the *First Folio* (1623), had

Pembroke as its patron. Pembroke was also the son of Henry Herbert, patron of the Pembroke's Men acting company – a possible employer of the young Shakespeare.

There are references to patronage throughout Shakespeare's sonnets and these two men therefore reflect this. In addition, each man was said to have refused to marry a prospective bride – Southampton in 1590 and Pembroke in 1595 – and this suits the pleas of Sonnets 1–17.

Nonetheless, there have been many valid reasons suggesting why neither of these two earls is the dedicatee and there have been many other proposals for the 'real' identity of Mr W.H. There were many prominent figures of the time with the same initials and there is also a good case to suggest that he must have been a 'William' like the poet himself, not least because of the 'Will-Sonnets' (135 and 136), where the word 'will' appears 19 times.

Wild speculation has led commentators who do not see Mr W.H. as synonymous with the youth to wonder whether the latter may have been another courtier, such as the Earl of Essex (close friend of the Earl of Southampton and a favourite of the Queen), Hamnet (Shakespeare's son) or even Elizabeth I herself.

The quest of finding an identity for the youth has led to the most contentious theory of all: that Shakespeare was a homosexual. After all, the word 'lover' is often used with reference to the young male friend, as are various sexual images, puns and innuendos. However, if we are to place the sonnet sequence into their historical context, it seems that the Early Modern word 'lover' did not always carry sexual connotations, while the said erotic imagery and wordplay was commonplace in all sonnet sequences to be directed at both men and women. Indeed, many modern academics view the relationship between the poet and the youth as homoerotic, rather than homosexual: the former being based upon erotically – not directly sexually – charged emotions, aroused by persons of one's own sex.

More to the point, male sexual intercourse is nowhere directly mentioned in Shakespeare's sonnets, with Sonnet 20 actually denying any interest in the matter whatsoever. As the poet's 'master-mistress' (line 2), the youth has the same beauty as a woman would have: the same complexion, but painted by Nature and not artifice; the same 'gentle heart', but more faithful and less changeable; the same bright eye, but less fickle and false. He has all the best parts that a woman has, with none of the negative qualities. Indeed, we almost forget him to be a man until there is mention of the 'one thing' (line 12) that has been added to his physical attributes. And yet, the poet insists that the youth's penis is 'to my purpose nothing' (line 12), as Nature has 'picked thee out' (line 13) for herself and her own sex's sexual purposes.

The dark lady

As many nominees have been proposed for the identity of the dark lady as for the youth, not least because – taking an autobiographical approach – the answer would 'prove' that Shakespeare was a heterosexual. Among the candidates are:

- Mary Fitton (1578–1647), who was maid of honour to the Queen. This married woman was mistress to William Herbert, Earl of Pembroke, bearing his child and ruining her reputation. Banished from the court, she went on to marry twice more. Critics of Fitton being the lady of the sonnets remind us that she was fair-complexioned, with brown hair and grey eyes.
- Aemilia Lanyer (1570–1654), who was married to the court musician, Alphonse, while being mistress to the theatrical patron, Henry Carey, Lord Hunsdon. She may well have known Shakespeare through her husband's court entertainment connections. It was the astrologer, Simon Forman, who wrote of her as an 'incuba', meaning that she was witch-like.
- Lucy Morgan, who was lady-in-waiting to the Queen, before becoming the madam of a brothel.
- William Davenant's mother. Davenant (1606–68) was an English poet, playwright and theatrical entrepreneur, who was very powerful in the theatrical world in the 1660s and it was he who was rumoured to be Shakespeare's illegitimate son.

Each one of these historical figures led a very exciting life of intrigue and this has only served to provide a series of flamboyant stories to attach to the mysterious figure of Shakespeare's dark lady.

The rival poet

It becomes clear that the youth and the dark lady are inextricably bound when it comes to their 'identification'; and the introduction of the rival poet only serves to add to the dilemma. Alluded to in Sonnets 76–86, the rival poet is the third mysterious individual in Shakespeare's poems. Speaking of him as 'a worthier pen' (Sonnet 79:6) and 'a better spirit' (Sonnet 80:2), by comparison the narrator, as poet, is 'inferior far' (Sonnet 80:7).

Commentators have simply identified Shakespeare's own poetic contemporaries as the rival, with candidates covering Christopher Marlowe, George Peele (c. 1557–96), Thomas Nashe (1567–c. 1601), Robert Greene (1558–92), Edmund Spenser, George Chapman (c. 1559–1634) and Ben Jonson, to name but a few.

Old theories will come again and new ones will be presented. No matter: the three characters will probably always remain an enigma. Real or fictitious, they are each of them witty and fascinating constructs by which Shakespeare carried his sonnet sequence.

Analysing the sonnet form

The birth of the sonnet

The sonnet's name originates from the thirteenth-century Italian, 'a little poem'. It is a lyric poem in a single stanza consisting of 14 iambic pentameter lines. Dante (1265–1321) was the first well-known sonneteer, followed by Petrarch (1304–74). Both chose to divide the sonnet into an octave (eight lines), rhyming *abba abba*, and a sestet (six lines) in which several rhyme schemes were permitted.

In 1527, Sir Thomas Wyatt (1503–42) visited Italy and brought the sonnet form to England, slightly varying the rhyme scheme to *abba abba cdd cee*. He continued the Italian tradition of stating a problem or issue in the octave and then attempting a resolution in the sestet.

Henry Howard (1517–47), the Earl of Surrey, went on to experiment with this 'Italian' sonnet form and to develop the 'English' or 'Shakespearean' sonnet. The stanza is broken into three quatrains and a concluding couplet with an *abab cdcd efef gg* rhyme scheme. This was seen to work much better for English sonneteers, since there are fewer words that rhyme in the English language than in the Italian. The three quatrains can repeat a problem or issue, with the option of changing tone or content slightly, while the final couplet can point an idea home with a concluding flourish or an epigrammatic (clever or amusing) turn.

Using Petrarch as their example, many Elizabethan poets wrote sonnet sequences, where sonnets are seen to be linked together by the numerous wrangles taking place in a romantic plot. Philip Sidney did this in his *Astrophel and Stella* (1580), while Edmund Spenser did the same in his *Amoretti* (1595). Indeed, Spenser was seen to develop his own sonnet form, in which he links each quatrain to the next by an interweaving rhyme scheme: *abab bcbc cdcd ee*.

Francesco Petrarca was born on 20 July 1304 in Arezzo, Italy and he was said to be the father of the Italian sonnet. His collection of 366 poems, the *Canzoniere* (or *Rime sparse*), dealt with his unrequited love for 'Laura'. Laura represented an ideal of womanhood, as both mistress and saint. Petrarch's love poems were full of romantic conceits, praising the lady's limitless accomplishments, her spiritual beauty and, of course, her physical perfection. In sonnet 157, Petrarch writes:

> Her head was fine gold, her face warm snow,
> Ebony her eyebrows, and her eyes two stars whence
> Love never bent his bow in vain;
> Pearls and crimson roses, where gathered sorrow
> Formed ardent beautiful words;
> Her sighs flame, her tears crystal.

Quite simply, Laura is a symbol of perfection: an icon. Leonard Forster's text, *The Icy Fire*, explains that the female's body parts are each representative of something beautiful or wholesome:

> Before the end of the fifteenth century in Italy the lady's beauties were codified – the golden hair, the fine white hands, the black eyes, the ebony eyebrows, the roses and lilies in her cheeks, her pearly teeth, her coral lips, her breasts like globes of alabaster. (1969, p.10)

In other words, the hair and teeth are valued beyond compare, the complexion untainted by the sun, the cheeks a reflection of the flower that the woman is, the lips as rarely red as coral and the breasts geometrically spherical. The eyes are always described as shining like the sun, being as deep and unfathomable as wells, while the eyebrows are drawn like Cupid's bows to remind the reader of the poet's love quest. Because Laura never requited the poet's love, she can be seen to indulge in a cold and controlling power over him; meanwhile, the poet is left only to contemplate his life while considering death.

Petrarchism was pervasive, but flexible, during the Early Modern period. Many poets followed it religiously, while others picked up certain ideas for use alongside their own. The ancient theory of physiognomy (the art of judging character or inner being from facial features or outward appearance) complemented Petrarchan thought, as it dictated that the outer body is a reflection of the inner soul: such that the beautiful Laura has a moral beauty within. Petrarch's principal theme was that outer beauty and inner beauty are comparable and this influenced the very young Shakespeare's writing as a both a poet and dramatist.

In one of his earliest dramatic works – *The Two Gentlemen of Verona* (c. 1590) – the line from the song 'Beauty lives with kindness' (Act IV, Scene 2, line 44) shows his acknowledgement of the theory of physiognomy and the idea of natural goodness.

In his sonnets, Shakespeare utilized the idea in the first lines to his opening poem, drawing upon the belief that breeding from the best stock will ensure beautiful offspring:

> **From fairest creatures we desire increase,**
> **That thereby beauty's rose might never die** (1–2)

However, as the sonnets continue we see Shakespeare relying on his readers' familiarity with the basic premise of physiognomy, such that its power is undermined. In terms of the beautiful youth, it soon becomes apparent that his physical appearance is incompatible with his soul. In other words, his beauty enables him to take advantage of his form so that he can hide his less beautiful inner self. The poet admits to falling prey to the youth's beauty, and thereby his plots, despite knowing full well that the outer bodily messages are incompatible with the inner. In terms of the dark lady, while there is no mismatch between her outer appearance and inner being, we see Shakespeare deliberately moving away from convention by painting her as the physical opposite of the Petrarchan figure.

To conclude

At their very heart, Shakespeare's sonnets are about love – and, more specifically, about a love triangle. The apparent narrative, demanding language, intriguing themes and points of contextual interest merge to create a sequence that is nothing short of compelling. When presented with this catalogue of stormy passions and violent emotions, which serve to mark out the central characters as complex, interesting and elusive, we cannot help but be driven on to further investigation.

The next section presents Shakespeare's 154 sonnet sequence in the order in which they were published for the very first time. As well as enjoying the read, it is important that you consider your own opinions and judgements throughout. With a text as old as Shakespeare's, there are bound to be many interpretations. While we are going to consider these, it is vital that you have the confidence to view your own ideas to be of equal value.

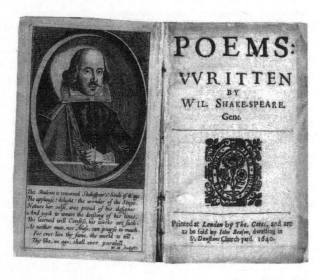

The title page and facing portrait of the 1640 edition of Shakespeare's poems

Shakespeare: The Complete Sonnets

1   From fairest creatures we desire increase,
    That thereby beauty's rose might never die,
    But as the riper should by time decease,
    His tender heir might bear his memory:
5   But thou, contracted to thine own bright eyes,
    Feed'st thy light's flame with self-substantial fuel,
    Making a famine where abundance lies,
    Thy self thy foe, to thy sweet self too cruel.
    Thou that art now the world's fresh ornament,
10 And only herald to the gaudy spring,
    Within thine own bud buriest thy content,
    And, tender churl, mak'st waste in niggarding:
      Pity the world, or else this glutton be,
      To eat the world's due, by the grave and thee.

2   When forty winters shall besiege thy brow,
    And dig deep trenches in thy beauty's field,
    Thy youth's proud livery so gazed on now
    Will be a tattered weed of small worth held:
5   Then, being asked where all thy beauty lies,
    Where all the treasure of thy lusty days,
    To say within thine own deep-sunken eyes
    Were an all-eating shame, and thriftless praise.
    How much more praise deserved thy beauty's use
10 If thou couldst answer 'This fair child of mine
    Shall sum my count, and make my old excuse',
    Proving his beauty by succession thine.
      This were to be new made when thou art old,
      And see thy blood warm when thou feel'st it cold.

3   Look in thy glass and tell the face thou viewest
      Now is the time that face should form another,
      Whose fresh repair if now thou not renewest
      Thou dost beguile the world, unbless some mother.
5   For where is she so fair whose uneared womb
      Disdains the tillage of thy husbandry?
      Or who is he so fond will be the tomb
      Of his self-love to stop posterity?
      Thou art thy mother's glass, and she in thee
10 Calls back the lovely April of her prime;
      So thou through windows of thine age shalt see,
      Despite of wrinkles, this thy golden time.
         But if thou live rememb'red not to be,
         Die single, and thine image dies with thee.

4   Unthrifty loveliness, why dost thou spend
      Upon thyself thy beauty's legacy?
      Nature's bequest gives nothing, but doth lend,
      And being frank she lends to those are free:
5   Then, beauteous niggard, why dost thou abuse
      The bounteous largess given thee to give?
      Profitless usurer, why dost thou use
      So great a sum of sums yet canst not live?
      For having traffic with thyself alone
10 Thou of thyself thy sweet self dost deceive.
      Then how, when nature calls thee to be gone,
      What acceptable audit canst thou leave?
         Thy unused beauty must be tombed with thee,
         Which usèd lives th' executor to be.

5 Those hours, that with gentle work did frame
The lovely gaze where every eye doth dwell,
Will play the tyrants to the very same,
And that un-fair which fairly doth excel:
5 For never-resting Time leads summer on
To hideous winter, and confounds him there,
Sap checked with frost and lusty leaves quite gone,
Beauty o'er-snowed and bareness everywhere.
Then, were not summer's distillation left
10 A liquid prisoner pent in walls of glass,
Beauty's effect with beauty were bereft,
Nor it nor no remembrance what it was.
    But flowers distilled, though they with winter meet,
    Lose but their show; their substance still lives sweet.

6 Then let not winter's ragged hand deface
In thee thy summer ere thou be distilled:
Make sweet some vial; treasure thou some place
With beauty's treasure ere it be self-killed:
5 That use is not forbidden usury
Which happies those that pay the willing loan;
That's for thyself to breed another thee,
Or ten times happier be it ten for one:
Ten times thyself were happier than thou art,
10 If ten of thine ten times refigured thee.
Then what could death do if thou shouldst depart,
Leaving thee living in posterity?
    Be not self-willed, for thou art much too fair
    To be death's conquest and make worms thine heir.

7 Lo in the orient when the gracious light
  Lifts up his burning head, each under-eye
  Doth homage to his new-appearing sight,
  Serving with looks his sacred majesty;
5 And having climbed the steep-up heavenly hill,
  Resembling strong youth in his middle age,
  Yet mortal looks adore his beauty still,
  Attending on his golden pilgrimage:
  But when from highmost pitch, with weary car,
10 Like feeble age he reeleth from the day,
  The eyes (fore duteous) now converted are
  From his low tract and look another way:
     So thou, thyself outgoing in thy noon,
     Unlooked on diest unless thou get a son.

8 Music to hear, why hear'st thou music sadly?
  Sweets with sweets war not, joy delights in joy:
  Why lov'st thou that which thou receiv'st not gladly,
  Or else receiv'st with pleasure thine annoy?
5 If the true concord of well-tunèd sounds
  By unions married do offend thine ear,
  They do but sweetly chide thee, who confounds
  In singleness the parts that thou shouldst bear.
  Mark how one string, sweet husband to another,
10 Strikes each in each by mutual ordering;
  Resembling sire, and child, and happy mother,
  Who all in one, one pleasing note do sing:
     Whose speechless song being many, seeming one,
     Sings this to thee, 'Thou single wilt prove none.'

9   Is it for fear to wet a widow's eye
    That thou consum'st thyself in single life?
    Ah, if thou issueless shalt hap to die
    The world will wail thee like a makeless wife.
5   The world will be thy widow and still weep
    That thou no form of thee hast left behind,
    When every private widow well may keep,
    By children's eyes, her husband's shape in mind.
    Look what an unthrift in the world doth spend
10 Shifts but his place, for still the world enjoys it;
    But beauty's waste hath in the world an end,
    And kept unused the user so destroys it:
      No love toward others in that bosom sits
      That on himself such murd'rous shame commits.

10 For shame deny that thou bear'st love to any,
    Who for thyself art so unprovident.
    Grant, if thou wilt, thou art beloved of many,
    But that thou none lov'st is most evident:
5   For thou art so possessed with murd'rous hate
    That 'gainst thyself thou stick'st not to conspire,
    Seeking that beauteous roof to ruinate,
    Which to repair should be thy chief desire.
    O, change thy thought, that I may change my mind:
10 Shall hate be fairer lodged than gentle love?
    Be as thy presence is, gracious and kind,
    Or to thyself at least kind-hearted prove:
      Make thee another self for love of me,
      That beauty still may live in thine or thee.

11 As fast as thou shalt wane, so fast thou grow'st
    In one of thine, from that which thou departest,
    And that fresh blood which youngly thou bestow'st
    Thou mayst call thine, when thou from youth
          convertest.
 5 Herein lives wisdom, beauty, and increase;
    Without this, folly, age, and cold decay.
    If all were minded so the times should cease,
    And threescore year would make the world away.
    Let those whom Nature hath not made for store,
10 Harsh, featureless, and rude, barrenly perish.
    Look whom she best endowed she gave the more,
    Which bounteous gift thou shouldst in bounty
          cherish.
      She carved thee for her seal, and meant thereby
      Thou shouldst print more, not let that copy die.

12 When I do count the clock that tells the time,
    And see the brave day sunk in hideous night;
    When I behold the violet past prime,
    And sable curls all silvered o'er with white;
 5 When lofty trees I see barren of leaves,
    Which erst from heat did canopy the herd,
    And summer's green all girded up in sheaves,
    Borne on the bier with white and bristly beard:
    Then of thy beauty do I question make,
10 That thou among the wastes of time must go,
    Since sweets and beauties do themselves forsake,
    And die as fast as they see others grow,
      And nothing 'gainst Time's scythe can make
          defence
      Save breed to brave him when he takes thee hence.

13 O that you were yourself; but, love, you are
   No longer yours than you yourself here live.
   Against this coming end you should prepare,
   And your sweet semblance to some other give.
5 So should that beauty which you hold in lease
   Find no determination; then you were
   Yourself again after your self's decease,
   When your sweet issue your sweet form should bear.
   Who lets so fair a house fall to decay,
10 Which husbandry in honour might uphold
   Against the stormy gusts of winter's day
   And barren rage of death's eternal cold?
       O none but unthrifts, dear my love, you know:
       You had a father, let your son say so.

14 Not from the stars do I my judgement pluck,
   And yet methinks I have astronomy,
   But not to tell of good or evil luck,
   Of plagues, of dearths, or seasons' quality;
5 Nor can I fortune to brief minutes tell,
   Pointing to each his thunder, rain, and wind,
   Or say with princes if it shall go well
   By oft predict that I in heaven find.
   But from thine eyes my knowledge I derive,
10 And, constant stars, in them I read such art
   As truth and beauty shall together thrive
   If from thyself to store thou wouldst convert:
       Or else of thee this I prognosticate,
       Thy end is truth's and beauty's doom and date.

15 When I consider every thing that grows
  Holds in perfection but a little moment;
  That this huge stage presenteth nought but shows,
  Whereon the stars in secret influence comment;
5 When I perceive that men as plants increase,
  Cheerèd and checked even by the selfsame sky,
  Vaunt in their youthful sap, at height decrease,
  And wear their brave state out of memory;
  Then the conceit of this inconstant stay
10 Sets you most rich in youth before my sight,
  Where wasteful time debateth with decay
  To change your day of youth to sullied night,
   And, all in war with Time for love of you,
   As he takes from you, I engraft you new.

16 But wherefore do not you a mightier way
  Make war upon this bloody tyrant Time,
  And fortify yourself in your decay
  With means more blessèd than my barren rhyme?
5 Now stand you on the top of happy hours,
  And many maiden gardens, yet unset,
  With virtuous wish would bear your living flowers,
  Much liker than your painted counterfeit:
  So should the lines of life that life repair,
10 Which this time's pencil or my pupil pen
  Neither in inward worth nor outward fair
  Can make you live yourself in eyes of men:
   To give away yourself keeps your self still,
   And you must live drawn by your own sweet skill.

17 Who will believe my verse in time to come
    If it were filled with your most high deserts?
    Though yet, heaven knows, it is but as a tomb
    Which hides your life, and shows not half your parts.
 5 If I could write the beauty of your eyes,
    And in fresh numbers number all your graces,
    The age to come would say 'This poet lies:
    Such heavenly touches ne'er touched earthly faces.'
    So should my papers (yellowed with their age)
10 Be scorned, like old men of less truth than tongue,
    And your true rights be termed a poet's rage,
    And stretchèd metre of an antique song.
        But were some child of yours alive that time,
        You should live twice, in it, and in my rhyme.

18 Shall I compare thee to a summer's day?
    Thou art more lovely and more temperate:
    Rough winds do shake the darling buds of May,
    And summer's lease hath all too short a date;
 5 Sometime too hot the eye of heaven shines,
    And often is his gold complexion dimmed,
    And every fair from fair sometime declines,
    By chance or nature's changing course untrimmed:
    But thy eternal summer shall not fade,
10 Nor lose possession of that fair thou ow'st;
    Nor shall Death brag thou wand'rest in his shade,
    When in eternal lines to time thou grow'st.
        So long as men can breathe or eyes can see,
        So long lives this, and this gives life to thee.

19   Devouring Time, blunt thou the lion's paws,
     And make the earth devour her own sweet brood,
     Pluck the keen teeth from the fierce tiger's jaws,
     And burn the long-lived phoenix in her blood,
5   Make glad and sorry seasons as thou fleet'st,
     And do whate'er thou wilt, swift-footed Time,
     To the wide world and all her fading sweets:
     But I forbid thee one most heinous crime,
     O carve not with thy hours my love's fair brow,
10 Nor draw no lines there with thine antique pen.
     Him in thy course untainted do allow
     For beauty's pattern to succeeding men.
       Yet do thy worst, old Time: despite thy wrong,
       My love shall in my verse ever live young.

20   A woman's face with nature's own hand painted,
     Hast thou, the master mistress of my passion;
     A woman's gentle heart, but not acquainted
     With shifting change as is false women's fashion;
5   An eye more bright than theirs, less false in rolling,
     Gilding the object whereupon it gazeth;
     A man in hue, all hues in his controlling,
     Which steals men's eyes and women's souls amazeth.
     And for a woman wert thou first created,
10 Till Nature as she wrought thee fell a-doting,
     And by addition me of thee defeated,
     By adding one thing to my purpose nothing.
       But since she pricked thee out for women's
          pleasure,
       Mine be thy love, and thy love's use their treasure.

21 So is it not with me as with that Muse,
    Stirred by a painted beauty to his verse,
    Who heaven itself for ornament doth use,
    And every fair with his fair doth rehearse,
5   Making a couplement of proud compare
    With sun and moon, with earth, and sea's rich gems,
    With April's first-born flowers, and all things rare
    That heaven's air in this huge rondure hems.
    O let me, true in love, but truly write,
10 And then, believe me, my love is as fair
    As any mother's child, though not so bright
    As those gold candles fixed in heaven's air:
        Let them say more that like of hearsay well:
        I will not praise, that purpose not to sell.

22 My glass shall not persuade me I am old,
    So long as youth and thou are of one date,
    But when in thee time's furrows I behold,
    Then look I death my days should expiate.
5   For all that beauty that doth cover thee
    Is but the seemly raiment of my heart,
    Which in thy breast doth live, as thine in me.
    How can I then be elder than thou art?
    O therefore, love, be of thyself so wary
10 As I, not for myself, but for thee will,
    Bearing thy heart which I will keep so chary
    As tender nurse her babe from faring ill.
        Presume not on thy heart when mine is slain:
        Thou gav'st me thine not to give back again.

23 As an unperfect actor on the stage,
    Who with his fear is put besides his part,
    Or some fierce thing replete with too much rage,
    Whose strength's abundance weakens his own heart;
5   So I, for fear of trust, forget to say
    The perfect ceremony of love's rite,
    And in mine own love's strength seem to decay,
    O'er-charged with burden of mine own love's might:
    O let my books be then the eloquence
10 And dumb presagers of my speaking breast,
    Who plead for love, and look for recompense,
    More than that tongue that more hath more
        expressed.
        O learn to read what silent love hath writ:
        To hear with eyes belongs to love's fine wit.

24 Mine eye hath played the painter and hath stelled
    Thy beauty's form in table of my heart;
    My body is the frame wherein 'tis held,
    And perspective it is best painter's art,
5   For through the painter must you see his skill
    To find where your true image pictured lies,
    Which in my bosom's shop is hanging still,
    That hath his windows glazèd with thine eyes.
    Now see what good turns eyes for eyes have done:
10 Mine eyes have drawn thy shape, and thine for me
    Are windows to my breast, wherethrough the sun
    Delights to peep, to gaze therein on thee.
    Yet eyes this cunning want to grace their art:
    They draw but what they see, know not the heart.

25 Let those who are in favour with their stars
     Of public honour and proud titles boast,
     Whilst I, whom fortune of such triumph bars,
     Unlooked for joy in that I honour most.
 5   Great princes' favourites their fair leaves spread
     But as the marigold at the sun's eye,
     And in themselves their pride lies burièd,
     For at a frown they in their glory die.
     The painful warrior famousèd for might
10   After a thousand victories, once foiled
     Is from the book of honour razèd quite,
     And all the rest forgot for which he toiled:
         Then happy I that love and am beloved
         Where I may not remove, nor be removed.

26 Lord of my love, to whom in vassalage
     Thy merit hath my duty strongly knit,
     To thee I send this written ambassage
     To witness duty, not to show my wit;
 5   Duty so great, which wit so poor as mine
     May make seem bare, in wanting words to show it,
     But that I hope some good conceit of thine
     In thy soul's thought (all naked) will bestow it,
     Till whatsoever star that guides my moving
10   Points on me graciously with fair aspect,
     And puts apparel on my tattered loving
     To show me worthy of thy sweet respect.
         Then may I dare to boast how I do love thee;
         Till then, not show my head where thou mayst
             prove me.

27   Weary with toil, I haste me to my bed,
      The dear repose for limbs with travail tirèd,
      But then begins a journey in my head
      To work my mind, when body's work's expirèd.
  5   For then my thoughts (from far, where I abide)
      Intend a zealous pilgrimage to thee,
      And keep my drooping eyelids open wide,
      Looking on darkness which the blind do see;
      Save that my soul's imaginary sight
 10   Presents thy shadow to my sightless view,
      Which like a jewel (hung in ghastly night)
      Makes black Night beauteous, and her old face new.
          Lo, thus by day my limbs, by night my mind,
          For thee, and for myself, no quiet find.

28   How can I then return in happy plight,
      That am debarred the benefit of rest,
      When day's oppression is not eased by night,
      But day by night and night by day oppressed?
  5   And each (though enemies to either's reign)
      Do in consent shake hands to torture me,
      The one by toil, the other to complain
      How far I toil, still farther off from thee.
      I tell the day to please him thou art bright,
 10   And dost him grace when clouds do blot the heaven;
      So flatter I the swart-complexioned night,
      When sparkling stars twire not thou gild'st the even.
          But day doth daily draw my sorrows longer,
          And night doth nightly make grief's length seem
              stronger.

29 When in disgrace with Fortune and men's eyes
  I all alone beweep my outcast state,
  And trouble deaf heaven with my bootless cries,
  And look upon myself and curse my fate,
 5 Wishing me like to one more rich in hope,
  Featured like him, like him with friends possessed,
  Desiring this man's art, and that man's scope,
  With what I most enjoy contented least;
  Yet in these thoughts myself almost despising,
10 Haply I think on thee, and then my state
  (Like to the lark at break of day arising)
  From sullen earth sings hymns at heaven's gate.
   For thy sweet love remembered such wealth brings
   That then I scorn to change my state with kings.

30 When to the sessions of sweet silent thought
  I summon up remembrance of things past,
  I sigh the lack of many a thing I sought,
  And with old woes new wail my dear time's waste;
 5 Then can I drown an eye (unused to flow)
  For precious friends hid in death's dateless night,
  And weep afresh love's long-since-cancelled woe,
  And moan th' expense of many a vanished sight;
  Then can I grieve at grievances fore-gone,
10 And heavily from woe to woe tell o'er
  The sad account of fore-bemoanèd moan,
  Which I new pay as if not paid before.
   But if the while I think on thee (dear friend)
   All losses are restored, and sorrows end.

31   Thy bosom is endearèd with all hearts
Which I by lacking have supposèd dead,
And there reigns Love and all Love's loving parts,
And all those friends which I thought burièd.
5   How many a holy and obsequious tear
Hath dear religious love stol'n from mine eye,
As interest of the dead, which now appear
But things removed that hidden in there lie?
Thou art the grave where buried love doth live,
10   Hung with the trophies of my lovers gone,
Who all their parts of me to thee did give;
That due of many, now is thine alone.
  Their images I loved I view in thee,
  And thou (all they) hast all the all of me.

32   If thou survive my well-contented day,
When that churl Death my bones with dust shall
      cover,
And shalt by fortune once more resurvey
These poor, rude lines of thy deceasèd lover,
5   Compare them with the bett'ring of the time,
And, though they be outstripped by every pen,
Reserve them for my love, not for their rhyme,
Exceeded by the height of happier men.
O then vouchsafe me but this loving thought:
10   'Had my friend's Muse grown with this growing age,
A dearer birth than this his love had brought,
To march in ranks of better equipage:
  But since he died, and poets better prove,
  Theirs for their style I'll read, his for his love.'

33 Full many a glorious morning have I seen
  Flatter the mountain tops with sovereign eye,
  Kissing with golden face the meadows green,
  Gilding pale streams with heavenly alchemy,
5 Anon permit the basest clouds to ride
  With ugly rack on his celestial face,
  And from the forlorn world his visage hide,
  Stealing unseen to west with this disgrace:
  Even so my sun one early morn did shine
10 With all triumphant splendour on my brow;
  But out alack, he was but one hour mine,
  The region cloud hath masked him from me now.
   Yet him for this my love no whit disdaineth:
   Suns of the world may stain, when heaven's sun
    staineth.

34 Why didst thou promise such a beauteous day,
  And make me travel forth without my cloak,
  To let base clouds o'ertake me in my way,
  Hiding thy brav'ry in their rotten smoke?
5 'Tis not enough that through the cloud thou break
  To dry the rain on my storm-beaten face,
  For no man well of such a salve can speak
  That heals the wound and cures not the disgrace;
  Nor can thy shame give physic to my grief:
10 Though thou repent, yet I have still the loss.
  Th' offender's sorrow lends but weak relief
  To him that bears the strong offence's cross.
   Ah, but those tears are pearl which thy love sheds,
   And they are rich, and ransom all ill deeds.

35   No more be grieved at that which thou hast done:
Roses have thorns, and silver fountains mud,
Clouds and eclipses stain both moon and sun,
And loathsome canker lives in sweetest bud.
5   All men make faults, and even I in this,
Authorizing thy trespass with compare,
Myself corrupting salving thy amiss,
Excusing thy sins more than thy sins are:
For to thy sensual fault I bring in sense –
10   Thy adverse party is thy advocate –
And 'gainst myself a lawful plea commence:
Such civil war is in my love and hate
   That I an accessary needs must be
   To that sweet thief which sourly robs from me.

36   Let me confess that we two must be twain,
Although our undivided loves are one:
So shall those blots that do with me remain,
Without thy help by me be borne alone.
5   In our two loves there is but one respect,
Though in our lives a separable spite,
Which, though it alter not love's sole effect,
Yet doth it steal sweet hours from love's delight.
I may not evermore acknowledge thee,
10   Lest my bewailèd guilt should do thee shame,
Nor thou with public kindness honour me,
Unless thou take that honour from thy name:
   But do not so; I love thee in such sort
   As thou being mine, mine is thy good report.

37 As a decrepit father takes delight
    To see his active child do deeds of youth,
    So I, made lame by Fortune's dearest spite,
    Take all my comfort of thy worth and truth.
5   For whether beauty, birth, or wealth, or wit,
    Or any of these all, or all, or more,
    Entitled in thy parts do crowned sit,
    I make my love engrafted to this store.
    So then I am not lame, poor, nor despised,
10 Whilst that this shadow doth such substance give
    That I in thy abundance am sufficed,
    And by a part of all thy glory live.
        Look what is best, that best I wish in thee;
        This wish I have, then ten times happy me.

38 How can my Muse want subject to invent,
    While thou dost breathe, that pour'st into my verse
    Thine own sweet argument, too excellent
    For every vulgar paper to rehearse?
5   O give thyself the thanks if aught in me
    Worthy perusal stand against thy sight,
    For who's so dumb that cannot write to thee,
    When thou thyself dost give invention light?
    Be thou the tenth Muse, ten times more in worth
10 Than those old nine which rhymers invocate;
    And he that calls on thee, let him bring forth
    Eternal numbers to outlive long date.
        If my slight Muse do please these curious days,
        The pain be mine, but thine shall be the praise.

39 O, how thy worth with manners may I sing,
When thou art all the better part of me?
What can mine own praise to mine own self bring,
And what is 't but mine own when I praise thee?
5 Even for this, let us divided live,
And our dear love lose name of single one,
That by this separation I may give
That due to thee which thou deserv'st alone.
O absence, what a torment wouldst thou prove,
10 Were it not thy sour leisure gave sweet leave
To entertain the time with thoughts of love,
Which time and thoughts so sweetly dost deceive;
    And that thou teachest how to make one twain,
    By praising him here who doth hence remain.

40 Take all my loves, my love, yea, take them all:
What hast thou then more than thou hadst before?
No love, my love, that thou mayst true love call:
All mine was thine before thou hadst this more.
5 Then if for my love thou my love receivest,
I cannot blame thee, for my love thou usest;
But yet be blamed, if thou this self deceivest
By wilful taste of what thyself refusest.
I do forgive thy robb'ry, gentle thief,
10 Although thou steal thee all my poverty;
And yet love knows it is a greater grief
To bear love's wrong than hate's known injury.
    Lascivious grace, in whom all ill well shows,
    Kill me with spites, yet we must not be foes.

41 Those pretty wrongs that liberty commits,
When I am sometime absent from thy heart,
Thy beauty and thy years full well befits,
For still temptation follows where thou art.
5 Gentle thou art, and therefore to be won;
Beauteous thou art, therefore to be assailèd.
And when a woman woos what woman's son
Will sourly leave her till he have prevailèd?
Ay me, but yet thou mightst my seat forbear,
10 And chide thy beauty and thy straying youth,
Who lead thee in their riot even there
Where thou art forced to break a two-fold truth:
　Hers, by thy beauty tempting her to thee,
　Thine, by thy beauty being false to me.

42 That thou hast her, it is not all my grief,
And yet it may be said I loved her dearly;
That she hath thee is of my wailing chief,
A loss in love that touches me more nearly.
5 Loving offenders, thus I will excuse ye:
Thou dost love her, because thou know'st I love her,
And for my sake even so doth she abuse me,
Suff'ring my friend for my sake to approve her.
If I lose thee, my loss is my love's gain;
10 And, losing her, my friend hath found that loss:
Both find each other, and I lose both twain,
And both for my sake lay on me this cross.
　But here's the joy: my friend and I are one.
　Sweet flatt'ry! Then she loves but me alone.

43 When most I wink, then do mine eyes best see,
    For all the day they view things unrespected,
    But when I sleep, in dreams they look on thee,
    And, darkly bright, are bright in dark directed.
5   Then thou, whose shadow shadows doth make
        bright,
    How would thy shadow's form form happy show,
    To the clear day with thy much clearer light,
    When to unseeing eyes thy shade shines so?
    How would (I say) mine eyes be blessèd made
10 By looking on thee in the living day,
    When in dead night thy fair imperfect shade
    Through heavy sleep on sightless eyes doth stay?
        All days are nights to see till I see thee,
        And nights bright days when dreams do show
            thee me.

44 If the dull substance of my flesh were thought,
    Injurious distance should not stop my way;
    For then, despite of space, I would be brought
    From limits far remote, where thou dost stay.
5   No matter then although my foot did stand
    Upon the farthest earth removed from thee,
    For nimble thought can jump both sea and land
    As soon as think the place where he would be.
    But ah, thought kills me that I am not thought,
10 To leap large lengths of miles when thou art gone,
    But that, so much of earth and water wrought,
    I must attend time's leisure with my moan,
        Receiving naught by elements so slow
        But heavy tears, badges of either's woe.

45   The other two, slight air and purging fire,
Are both with thee, wherever I abide:
The first my thought, the other my desire,
These present-absent with sweet motion slide.
5   For when these quicker elements are gone
In tender embassy of love to thee,
My life, being made of four, with two alone
Sinks down to death, oppressed with melancholy,
Until life's composition be recurèd
10   By those swift messengers returned from thee,
Who even but now come back again assurèd
Of thy fair health, recounting it to me.
    This told, I joy; but then, no longer glad,
    I send them back again and straight grow sad.

46   Mine eye and heart are at a mortal war
How to divide the conquest of thy sight.
Mine eye my heart thy picture's sight would bar;
My heart, mine eye the freedom of that right.
5   My heart doth plead that thou in him dost lie
(A closet never pierced with crystal eyes),
But the defendant doth that plea deny,
And says in him thy fair appearance lies.
To 'cide this title is impanellèd
10   A quest of thoughts, all tenants to the heart,
And by their verdict is determinèd
The clear eye's moiety, and the dear heart's part,
    As thus: mine eye's due is thy outward part,
    And my heart's right thy inward love of heart.

47   Betwixt mine eye and heart a league is took,
       And each doth good turns now unto the other.
       When that mine eye is famished for a look,
       Or heart in love with sighs himself doth smother,
5   With my love's picture then my eye doth feast,
       And to the painted banquet bids my heart.
       Another time mine eye is my heart's guest,
       And in his thoughts of love doth share a part.
       So either by thy picture or my love,
10   Thyself away are present still with me;
       For thou not farther than my thoughts canst move,
       And I am still with them, and they with thee;
         Or if they sleep, thy picture in my sight
         Awakes my heart, to heart's and eye's delight.

48   How careful was I, when I took my way,
       Each trifle under truest bars to thrust,
       That to my use it might unusèd stay
       From hands of falsehood, in sure wards of trust?
5   But thou, to whom my jewels trifles are,
       Most worthy comfort, now my greatest grief,
       Thou best of dearest, and mine only care,
       Art left the prey of every vulgar thief.
       Thee have I not locked up in any chest,
10   Save where thou art not, though I feel thou art,
       Within the gentle closure of my breast,
       From whence at pleasure thou mayst come and part;
         And even thence thou wilt be stol'n, I fear:
         For truth proves thievish for a prize so dear.

49 Against that time (if ever that time come)
    When I shall see thee frown on my defects,
    Whenas thy love hath cast his utmost sum,
    Called to that audit by advised respects;
 5 Against that time when thou shalt strangely pass,
    And scarcely greet me with that sun, thine eye,
    When love, converted from the thing it was,
    Shall reasons find of settled gravity;
    Against that time do I ensconce me here,
10 Within the knowledge of mine own desert,
    And this my hand against myself uprear
    To guard the lawful reasons on thy part.
        To leave poor me thou hast the strength of laws,
        Since why to love I can allege no cause.

50 How heavy do I journey on the way,
    When what I seek (my weary travel's end)
    Doth teach that ease and that repose to say
    'Thus far the miles are measured from thy friend.'
 5 The beast that bears me, tirèd with my woe,
    Plods dully on, to bear that weight in me,
    As if by some instinct the wretch did know
    His rider loved not speed being made from thee.
    The bloody spur cannot provoke him on
10 That sometimes anger thrusts into his hide,
    Which heavily he answers with a groan
    More sharp to me than spurring to his side,
        For that same groan doth put this in my mind:
        My grief lies onward, and my joy behind.

51   Thus can my love excuse the slow offence
      Of my dull bearer, when from thee I speed:
      'From where thou art, why should I haste me thence?
      Till I return, of posting is no need.'
  5 O what excuse will my poor beast then find
      When swift extremity can seem but slow?
      Then should I spur, though mounted on the wind:
      In wingèd speed no motion shall I know.
      Then can no horse with my desire keep pace;
10 Therefore desire (of perfect'st love being made)
      Shall weigh no dull flesh in his fiery race,
      But love, for love, thus shall excuse my jade:
        'Since from thee going he went wilful slow,
        Towards thee I'll run, and give him leave to go.'

52   So am I as the rich, whose blessèd key
      Can bring him to his sweet up-lockèd treasure,
      The which he will not ev'ry hour survey
      For blunting the fine point of seldom pleasure.
  5 Therefore are feasts so solemn and so rare,
      Since, seldom coming, in the long year set
      Like stones of worth they thinly placèd are,
      Or captain jewels in the carcanet.
      So is the time that keeps you as my chest,
10 Or as the wardrobe which the robe doth hide
      To make some special instant special blest,
      By new unfolding his imprisoned pride.
        Blessèd are you whose worthiness gives scope,
        Being had, to triumph; being lacked, to hope.

53   What is your substance, whereof are you made,
That millions of strange shadows on you tend?
Since every one hath, every one, one shade,
And you, but one, can every shadow lend.
5   Describe Adonis, and the counterfeit
Is poorly imitated after you.
On Helen's cheek all art of beauty set,
And you in Grecian tires are painted new.
Speak of the spring and foison of the year,
10   The one doth shadow of your beauty show,
The other as your bounty doth appear,
And you in every blessèd shape we know.
    In all external grace you have some part,
    But you like none, none you, for constant heart.

54   O how much more doth beauty beauteous seem
By that sweet ornament which truth doth give.
The rose looks fair, but fairer we it deem
For that sweet odour which doth in it live.
5   The canker-blooms have full as deep a dye
As the perfumèd tincture of the roses,
Hang on such thorns, and play as wantonly
When summer's breath their maskèd buds discloses;
But, for their virtue only is their show,
10   They live unwooed, and unrespected fade,
Die to themselves. Sweet roses do not so;
Of their sweet deaths are sweetest odours made:
    And so of you, beauteous and lovely youth:
    When that shall vade, by verse distils your truth.

55   Not marble, nor the gilded monuments
      Of princes shall outlive this pow'rful rhyme,
      But you shall shine more bright in these contents
      Than unswept stone besmeared with sluttish time.
5   When wasteful war shall statues overturn,
      And broils root out the work of masonry,
      Nor Mars his sword, nor war's quick fire shall burn
      The living record of your memory.
      'Gainst death, and all oblivious enmity
10   Shall you pace forth, your praise shall still find room,
      Even in the eyes of all posterity
      That wear this world out to the ending doom.
          So, till the judgement that yourself arise,
          You live in this, and dwell in lovers' eyes.

56   Sweet love, renew thy force. Be it not said
      Thy edge should blunter be than appetite,
      Which but today by feeding is allayed,
      Tomorrow sharpened in his former might.
5   So love be thou, although today thou fill
      Thy hungry eyes, even till they wink with fullness,
      Tomorrow see again, and do not kill
      The spirit of love with a perpetual dullness.
      Let this sad int'rim like the ocean be,
10   Which parts the shore where two, contracted new,
      Come daily to the banks, that when they see
      Return of love, more blest may be the view;
          Or call it winter, which being full of care,
          Makes summer's welcome thrice more wished,
              more rare.

57 Being your slave, what should I do but tend
    Upon the hours and times of your desire?
    I have no precious time at all to spend,
    Nor services to do, till you require.
5   Nor dare I chide the world-without-end hour
    Whilst I (my sovereign) watch the clock for you,
    Nor think the bitterness of absence sour
    When you have bid your servant once adieu.
    Nor dare I question with my jealous thought
10 Where you may be, or your affairs suppose,
    But like a sad slave stay and think of naught,
    Save where you are how happy you make those.
      So true a fool is love, that in your will,
      Though you do anything, he thinks no ill.

58 That god forbid, that made me first your slave,
    I should in thought control your times of pleasure,
    Or at your hand th' account of hours to crave,
    Being your vassal bound to stay your leisure.
5   O let me suffer (being at your beck)
    Th' imprisoned absence of your liberty,
    And, patience-tame to sufferance, bide each check
    Without accusing you of injury.
    Be where you list, your charter is so strong
10 That you yourself may privilege your time
    To what you will: to you it doth belong
    Yourself to pardon of self-doing crime.
      I am to wait, though waiting so be hell,
      Not blame your pleasure be it ill or well.

59 If there be nothing new, but that which is
Hath been before, how are our brains beguiled,
Which, labouring for invention, bear amiss
The second burden of a former child?
5 O that record could with a backward look,
Even of five hundred courses of the sun,
Show me your image in some antique book,
Since mind at first in character was done,
That I might see what the old world could say
10 To this composèd wonder of your frame;
Whether we are mended, or whe'er better they,
Or whether revolution be the same.
 O, sure I am the wits of former days
 To subjects worse have given admiring praise.

60 Like as the waves make towards the pebbled shore,
So do our minutes hasten to their end,
Each changing place with that which goes before,
In sequent toil all forwards do contend.
5 Nativity, once in the main of light,
Crawls to maturity, wherewith being crowned
Crookèd eclipses 'gainst his glory fight,
And Time that gave doth now his gift confound.
Time doth transfix the flourish set on youth,
10 And delves the parallels in beauty's brow,
Feeds on the rarities of nature's truth,
And nothing stands but for his scythe to mow.
 And yet to times in hope my verse shall stand,
 Praising thy worth, despite his cruel hand.

61 Is it thy will thy image should keep open
My heavy eyelids to the weary night?
Dost thou desire my slumbers should be broken,
While shadows like to thee do mock my sight?
5 Is it thy spirit that thou send'st from thee
So far from home into my deeds to pry,
To find out shames and idle hours in me,
The scope and tenure of thy jealousy?
O no, thy love, though much, is not so great:
10 It is my love that keeps mine eye awake,
Mine own true love that doth my rest defeat,
To play the watchman ever for thy sake.
    For thee watch I, whilst thou dost wake elsewhere,
    From me far off, with others all too near.

62 Sin of self-love possesseth all mine eye,
And all my soul, and all my every part;
And for this sin there is no remedy,
It is so grounded inward in my heart.
5 Methinks no face so gracious is as mine,
No shape so true, no truth of such account,
And for myself mine own worth do define
As I all other in all worths surmount.
But when my glass shows me myself indeed,
10 Beated and chapped with tanned antiquity,
Mine own self-love quite contrary I read;
Self so self-loving were iniquity:
    'Tis thee (my self) that for myself I praise,
    Painting my age with beauty of thy days.

63   Against my love shall be as I am now,
With Time's injurious hand crushed and o'er-worn,
When hours have drained his blood and filled his
       brow
With lines and wrinkles, when his youthful morn
5   Hath travelled on to age's steepy night,
And all those beauties whereof now he's king
Are vanishing, or vanished out of sight,
Stealing away the treasure of his spring:
For such a time do I now fortify
10 Against confounding age's cruel knife,
That he shall never cut from memory
My sweet love's beauty, though my lover's life.
    His beauty shall in these black lines be seen,
    And they shall live, and he in them, still green.

64   When I have seen by Time's fell hand defacèd
The rich proud cost of outworn buried age,
When sometime lofty towers I see down razèd
And brass eternal slave to mortal rage;
5   When I have seen the hungry ocean gain
Advantage on the kingdom of the shore,
And the firm soil win of the wat'ry main,
Increasing store with loss, and loss with store;
When I have seen such interchange of state,
10 Or state itself confounded to decay,
Ruin hath taught me thus to ruminate,
That Time will come and take my love away.
    This thought is as a death, which cannot choose
    But weep to have that which it fears to lose.

65   Since brass, nor stone, nor earth, nor boundless sea,
But sad mortality o'ersways their power,
How with this rage shall beauty hold a plea,
Whose action is no stronger than a flower?
5   O how shall summer's honey breath hold out
Against the wrackful siege of batt'ring days,
When rocks impregnable are not so stout,
Nor gates of steel so strong, but time decays?
O fearful meditation; where, alack,
10   Shall Time's best jewel from Time's chest lie hid?
Or what strong hand can hold his swift foot back,
Or who his spoil of beauty can forbid?
    O none, unless this miracle have might,
    That in black ink my love may still shine bright.

66   Tired with all these, for restful death I cry:
As to behold desert a beggar born,
And needy nothing trimmed in jollity,
And purest faith unhappily forsworn,
5   And gilded honour shamefully misplaced,
And maiden virtue rudely strumpeted,
And right perfection wrongfully disgraced,
And strength by limping sway disablèd,
And art made tongue-tied by authority,
10   And folly (doctor-like) controlling skill,
And simple truth miscalled simplicity,
And captive good attending captain ill.
    Tired with all these, from these would I be gone,
    Save that to die I leave my love alone.

67   Ah, wherefore with infection should he live,
     And with his presence grace impiety,
     That sin by him advantage should achieve
     And lace itself with his society?
5   Why should false painting imitate his cheek,
     And steal dead seeming of his living hue?
     Why should poor beauty indirectly seek
     Roses of shadow, since his rose is true?
     Why should he live, now Nature bankrupt is,
10 Beggared of blood to blush through lively veins,
     For she hath no exchequer now but his,
     And proud of many, lives upon his gains?
       O him she stores to show what wealth she had
       In days long since, before these last so bad.

68   Thus is his cheek the map of days outworn,
     When beauty lived and died as flowers do now,
     Before these bastard signs of fair were born,
     Or durst inhabit on a living brow:
5   Before the golden tresses of the dead,
     The right of sepulchres, were shorn away,
     To live a second life on second head,
     Ere beauty's dead fleece made another gay:
     In him these holy antique hours are seen
10 Without all ornament, itself and true,
     Making no summer of another's green,
     Robbing no old to dress his beauty new;
       And him as for a map doth Nature store,
       To show false Art what beauty was of yore.

69   Those parts of thee that the world's eye doth view
     Want nothing that the thought of hearts can mend:
     All tongues (the voice of souls) give thee that due,
     Utt'ring bare truth, even so as foes commend.
5   Thy outward thus with outward praise is crowned,
     But those same tongues that give thee so thine own
     In other accents do this praise confound
     By seeing farther than the eye hath shown.
     They look into the beauty of thy mind,
10 And that, in guess, they measure by thy deeds.
     Then, churls, their thoughts (although their eyes
           were kind)
     To thy fair flower add the rank smell of weeds.
       But why thy odour matcheth not thy show,
       The soil is this, that thou dost common grow.

70   That thou art blamed shall not be thy defect,
     For slander's mark was ever yet the fair.
     The ornament of beauty is suspect,
     A crow that flies in heaven's sweetest air.
5   So thou be good, slander doth but approve
     Thy worth the greater, being wooed of time.
     For canker vice the sweetest buds doth love,
     And thou present'st a pure unstainèd prime.
     Thou hast passed by the ambush of young days,
10 Either not assailed, or victor, being charged;
     Yet this thy praise cannot be so thy praise
     To tie up envy, evermore enlarged.
       If some suspect of ill masked not thy show
       Then thou alone kingdoms of hearts shouldst owe.

71 No longer mourn for me when I am dead
    Than you shall hear the surly sullen bell
    Give warning to the world that I am fled
    From this vile world with vilest worms to dwell:
5   Nay, if you read this line, remember not
    The hand that writ it, for I love you so
    That I in your sweet thoughts would be forgot,
    If thinking on me then should make you woe.
    O, if (I say) you look upon this verse
10 When I (perhaps) compounded am with clay,
    Do not so much as my poor name rehearse;
    But let your love even with my life decay,
        Lest the wise world should look into your moan
        And mock you with me after I am gone.

72 O, lest the world should task you to recite
    What merit lived in me that you should love
    After my death (dear love) forget me quite,
    For you in me can nothing worthy prove;
5   Unless you would devise some virtuous lie,
    To do more for me than mine own desert,
    And hang more praise upon deceasèd I
    Than niggard truth would willingly impart.
    O, lest your true love may seem false in this,
10 That you for love speak well of me untrue,
    My name be buried where my body is,
    And live no more to shame nor me, nor you.
        For I am shamed by that which I bring forth,
        And so should you, to love things nothing worth.

54

73   That time of year thou mayst in me behold
     When yellow leaves, or none, or few, do hang
     Upon those boughs which shake against the cold,
     Bare ruined choirs, where late the sweet birds sang.
5   In me thou seest the twilight of such day
     As after sunset fadeth in the west,
     Which by and by black night doth take away,
     Death's second self, that seals up all in rest.
     In me thou seest the glowing of such fire
10 That on the ashes of his youth doth lie,
     As the death-bed whereon it must expire,
     Consumed with that which it was nourished by.
       This thou perceiv'st, which makes thy love more
          strong,
       To love that well, which thou must leave ere long.

74   But be contented when that fell arrest
     Without all bail shall carry me away;
     My life hath in this line some interest,
     Which for memorial still with thee shall stay.
5   When thou reviewest this, thou dost review
     The very part was consecrate to thee.
     The earth can have but earth, which is his due;
     My spirit is thine, the better part of me.
     So then thou hast but lost the dregs of life,
10 The prey of worms, my body being dead,
     The coward conquest of a wretch's knife,
     Too base of thee to be rememberèd.
       The worth of that, is that which it contains,
       And that is this, and this with thee remains.

75 So are you to my thoughts as food to life,
    Or as sweet seasoned showers are to the ground;
    And for the peace of you I hold such strife
    As 'twixt a miser and his wealth is found:
 5 Now proud as an enjoyer, and anon
    Doubting the filching age will steal his treasure,
    Now counting best to be with you alone,
    Then bettered that the world may see my pleasure;
    Sometime all full with feasting on your sight,
10 And by and by clean starvèd for a look.
    Possessing or pursuing, no delight,
    Save what is had or must be from you took.
        Thus do I pine and surfeit day by day,
        Or gluttoning on all, or all away.

76 Why is my verse so barren of new pride,
    So far from variation or quick change?
    Why with the time do I not glance aside
    To new-found methods, and to compounds strange?
 5 Why write I still all one, ever the same,
    And keep invention in a noted weed,
    That every word doth almost tell my name,
    Showing their birth, and where they did proceed?
    O know, sweet love, I always write of you,
10 And you and love are still my argument;
    So all my best is dressing old words new,
    Spending again what is already spent:
        For as the sun is daily new and old,
        So is my love, still telling what is told.

77 Thy glass will show thee how thy beauties wear,
     Thy dial how thy precious minutes waste,
     The vacant leaves thy mind's imprint will bear,
     And of this book this learning mayst thou taste:
5   The wrinkles which thy glass will truly show
     Of mouthèd graves will give thee memory;
     Thou by thy dial's shady stealth mayst know
     Time's thievish progress to eternity.
     Look what thy memory cannot contain,
10 Commit to these waste blanks, and thou shalt find
     Those children nursed, delivered from thy brain,
     To take a new acquaintance of thy mind.
       These offices, so oft as thou wilt look,
       Shall profit thee, and much enrich thy book.

78 So oft have I invoked thee for my Muse
     And found such fair assistance in my verse
     As every alien pen hath got my use,
     And under thee their poesy disperse.
5   Thine eyes, that taught the dumb on high to sing,
     And heavy ignorance aloft to fly,
     Have added feathers to the learnèd's wing,
     And given grace a double majesty.
     Yet be most proud of that which I compile,
10 Whose influence is thine, and born of thee.
     In others' works thou dost but mend the style,
     And arts with thy sweet graces gracèd be;
       But thou art all my art, and dost advance
       As high as learning my rude ignorance.

79   Whilst I alone did call upon thy aid
      My verse alone had all thy gentle grace,
      But now my gracious numbers are decayed,
      And my sick Muse doth give another place.
5   I grant (sweet love) thy lovely argument
      Deserves the travail of a worthier pen,
      Yet what of thee thy poet doth invent
      He robs thee of, and pays it thee again.
      He lends thee virtue, and he stole that word
10 From thy behaviour; beauty doth he give
      And found it in thy cheek; he can afford
      No praise to thee but what in thee doth live.
         Then thank him not for that which he doth say,
         Since what he owes thee, thou thyself dost pay.

80   O, how I faint when I of you do write,
      Knowing a better spirit doth use your name,
      And in the praise thereof spends all his might
      To make me tongue-tied speaking of your fame.
5   But since your worth (wide as the ocean is)
      The humble as the proudest sail doth bear,
      My saucy barque (inferior far to his)
      On your broad main doth wilfully appear.
      Your shallowest help will hold me up afloat,
10 Whilst he upon your soundless deep doth ride;
      Or (being wrecked) I am a worthless boat,
      He of tall building, and of goodly pride.
         Then if he thrive and I be cast away,
         The worst was this, my love was my decay.

81 Or I shall live your epitaph to make,
Or you survive when I in earth am rotten,
From hence your memory death cannot take,
Although in me each part will be forgotten.
5 Your name from hence immortal life shall have,
Though I (once gone) to all the world must die.
The earth can yield me but a common grave
When you entombèd in men's eyes shall lie:
Your monument shall be my gentle verse,
10 Which eyes not yet created shall o'er-read,
And tongues-to-be your being shall rehearse,
When all the breathers of this world are dead.
  You still shall live (such virtue hath my pen)
    Where breath most breathes, even in the mouths
        of men.

82 I grant thou wert not married to my Muse,
And therefore mayst without attaint o'er-look
The dedicated words which writers use
Of their fair subject, blessing every book.
5 Thou art as fair in knowledge as in hue,
Finding thy worth a limit past my praise,
And therefore art enforced to seek anew
Some fresher stamp of the time-bettering days.
And do so, love; yet when they have devised
10 What strainèd touches rhetoric can lend,
Thou, truly fair, wert truly sympathized
In true, plain words, by thy true-telling friend.
  And their gross painting might be better used
    Where cheeks need blood: in thee it is abused.

83   I never saw that you did painting need,
     And therefore to your fair no painting set.
     I found (or thought I found) you did exceed
     The barren tender of a poet's debt;
5   And therefore have I slept in your report,
     That you yourself being extant might well show
     How far a modern quill doth come too short,
     Speaking of worth, what worth in you doth grow.
     This silence for my sin you did impute,
10 Which shall be most my glory, being dumb:
     For I impair not beauty, being mute,
     When others would give life, and bring a tomb.
       There lives more life in one of your fair eyes
       Than both your poets can in praise devise.

84   Who is it that says most, which can say more
     Than this rich praise: that you alone are you,
     In whose confine immurèd is the store
     Which should example where your equal grew?
5   Lean penury within that pen doth dwell,
     That to his subject lends not some small glory,
     But he that writes of you, if he can tell
     That you are you, so dignifies his story.
     Let him but copy what in you is writ,
10 Not making worse what nature made so clear,
     And such a counterpart shall fame his wit,
     Making his style admirèd everywhere.
       You to your beauteous blessings add a curse,
       Being fond on praise, which makes your praises
         worse.

85   My tongue-tied Muse in manners holds her still,
     While comments of your praise, richly compiled,
     Reserve their character with golden quill
     And precious phrase by all the Muses filed.
5   I think good thoughts, whilst other write good words,
     And like unlettered clerk still cry 'Amen'
     To every hymn that able spirit affords,
     In polished form of well-refinèd pen.
     Hearing you praised, I say ''Tis so, 'tis true',
10 And to the most of praise add something more,
     But that is in my thought, whose love to you
     (Though words come hindmost) holds his rank
        before.
       Then others for the breath of words respect;
       Me for my dumb thoughts, speaking in effect.

86   Was it the proud full sail of his great verse,
     Bound for the prize of all-too-precious you,
     That did my ripe thoughts in my brain inhearse,
     Making their tomb the womb wherein they grew?
5   Was it his spirit, by spirits taught to write
     Above a mortal pitch, that struck me dead?
     No, neither he, nor his compeers by night
     Giving him aid, my verse astonishèd.
     He, nor that affable familiar ghost
10 Which nightly gulls him with intelligence,
     As victors of my silence cannot boast:
     I was not sick of any fear from thence.
       But, when your countenance filled up his line,
       Then lacked I matter, that enfeebled mine.

87 Farewell, thou art too dear for my possessing,
    And like enough thou know'st thy estimate.
    The charter of thy worth gives thee releasing:
    My bonds in thee are all determinate.
5   For how do I hold thee but by thy granting,
    And for that riches where is my deserving?
    The cause of this fair gift in me is wanting,
    And so my patent back again is swerving.
    Thyself thou gav'st, thy own worth then not
            knowing,
10 Or me, to whom thou gav'st it, else mistaking;
    So thy great gift, upon misprision growing,
    Comes home again, on better judgement making.
        Thus have I had thee as a dream doth flatter:
        In sleep a king, but waking no such matter.

88 When thou shalt be disposed to set me light,
    And place my merit in the eye of scorn,
    Upon thy side against myself I'll fight,
    And prove thee virtuous, though thou art forsworn.
5   With mine own weakness being best acquainted,
    Upon thy part I can set down a story
    Of faults concealed, wherein I am attainted,
    That thou in losing me shall win much glory.
    And I by this will be a gainer too,
10 For bending all my loving thoughts on thee:
    The injuries that to myself I do,
    Doing thee vantage, double vantage me.
        Such is my love, to thee I so belong,
        That for thy right myself will bear all wrong.

89   Say that thou didst forsake me for some fault,
     And I will comment upon that offence.
     Speak of my lameness, and I straight will halt,
     Against thy reasons making no defence.
5   Thou canst not (love) disgrace me half so ill,
     To set a form upon desirèd change,
     As I'll myself disgrace, knowing thy will.
     I will acquaintance strangle and look strange,
     Be absent from thy walks, and in my tongue
10   Thy sweet belovèd name no more shall dwell,
     Lest I (too much profane) should do it wrong,
     And haply of our old acquaintance tell.
         For thee, against myself, I'll vow debate;
         For I must ne'er love him whom thou dost hate.

90   Then hate me when thou wilt, if ever, now,
     Now, while the world is bent my deeds to cross,
     Join with the spite of Fortune, make me bow,
     And do not drop in for an after-loss.
5   Ah do not, when my heart hath 'scaped this sorrow,
     Come in the rearward of a conquered woe;
     Give not a windy night a rainy morrow
     To linger out a purposed overthrow.
     If thou wilt leave me, do not leave me last,
10   When other petty griefs have done their spite,
     But in the onset come, so shall I taste
     At first the very worst of Fortune's might,
         And other strains of woe, which now seem woe,
         Compared with loss of thee, will not seem so.

91 Some glory in their birth, some in their skill,
    Some in their wealth, some in their body's force,
    Some in their garments, though new-fangled ill,
    Some in their hawks and hounds, some in their
        horse.
5   And every humour hath his adjunct pleasure
    Wherein it finds a joy above the rest;
    But these particulars are not my measure,
    All these I better in one general best.
    Thy love is better than high birth to me,
10 Richer than wealth, prouder than garments' cost,
    Of more delight than hawks or horses be:
    And, having thee, of all men's pride I boast,
        Wretched in this alone; that thou mayst take
        All this away, and me most wretched make.

92 But do thy worst to steal thyself away,
    For term of life thou art assurèd mine,
    And life no longer than thy love will stay,
    For it depends upon that love of thine.
5   Then need I not to fear the worst of wrongs,
    When in the least of them my life hath end.
    I see a better state to me belongs
    Than that which on thy humour doth depend.
    Thou canst not vex me with inconstant mind,
10 Since that my life on thy revolt doth lie.
    O, what a happy title do I find,
    Happy to have thy love, happy to die!
        But what's so blessèd fair that fears no blot?
        Thou mayst be false, and yet I know it not.

93 So shall I live, supposing thou art true,
    Like a deceivèd husband, so love's face
    May still seem love to me, though altered new:
    Thy looks with me, thy heart in other place.
5   For there can live no hatred in thine eye,
    Therefore in that I cannot know thy change.
    In many's looks the false heart's history
    Is writ in moods and frowns and wrinkles strange;
    But heaven in thy creation did decree
10 That in thy face sweet loves should ever dwell.
    Whate'er thy thoughts, or thy heart's workings be,
    Thy looks should nothing thence but sweetness tell.
        How like Eve's apple doth thy beauty grow,
        If thy sweet virtue answer not thy show.

94 They that have power to hurt and will do none,
    That do not do the thing they most do show,
    Who, moving others, are themselves as stone,
    Unmovèd, cold, and to temptation slow:
5   They rightly do inherit heaven's graces,
    And husband nature's riches from expense.
    They are the lords and owners of their faces,
    Others but stewards of their excellence.
    The summer's flower is to the summer sweet,
10 Though to itself it only live and die,
    But if that flower with base infection meet,
    The basest weed outbraves his dignity:
        For sweetest things turn sourest by their deeds;
        Lilies that fester smell far worse than weeds.

95   How sweet and lovely dost thou make the shame,
Which, like a canker in the fragrant rose,
Doth spot the beauty of thy budding name?
O, in what sweets dost thou thy sins enclose!
5 That tongue that tells the story of thy days
(Making lascivious comments on thy sport)
Cannot dispraise, but in a kind of praise,
Naming thy name blesses an ill report.
O, what a mansion have those vices got,
10 Which for their habitation chose out thee,
Where beauty's veil doth cover every blot,
And all things turns to fair that eyes can see!
    Take heed (dear heart) of this large privilege:
    The hardest knife ill-used doth lose his edge.

96   Some say thy fault is youth, some wantonness,
Some say thy grace is youth and gentle sport.
Both grace and faults are loved of more and less:
Thou mak'st faults graces, that to thee resort.
5 As on the finger of a thronèd queen
The basest jewel will be well esteemed,
So are those errors that in thee are seen
To truths translated, and for true things deemed.
How many lambs might the stern wolf betray,
10 If like a lamb he could his looks translate?
How many gazers mightst thou lead away,
If thou wouldst use the strength of all thy state?
    But do not so; I love thee in such sort
    As thou being mine, mine is thy good report.

97   How like a winter hath my absence been
      From thee, the pleasure of the fleeting year?
      What freezings have I felt, what dark days seen?
      What old December's bareness everywhere?
5   And yet this time removed was summer's time,
      The teeming autumn big with rich increase,
      Bearing the wanton burden of the prime,
      Like widowed wombs after their lords' decease:
      Yet this abundant issue seemed to me
10 But hope of orphans and unfathered fruit,
      For summer and his pleasures wait on thee,
      And thou away, the very birds are mute.
         Or if they sing, 'tis with so dull a cheer
         That leaves look pale, dreading the winter's near.

98   From you have I been absent in the spring,
      When proud-pied April (dressed in all his trim)
      Hath put a spirit of youth in every thing,
      That heavy Saturn laughed and leapt with him.
5   Yet nor the lays of birds, nor the sweet smell
      Of different flowers in odour and in hue,
      Could make me any summer's story tell,
      Or from their proud lap pluck them where they
         grew.
      Nor did I wonder at the lily's white,
10 Nor praise the deep vermilion in the rose;
      They were but sweet, but figures of delight
      Drawn after you, you pattern of all those.
         Yet seemed it winter still, and, you away,
         As with your shadow I with these did play.

99   The forward violet thus did I chide:
      'Sweet thief, whence did thou steal thy sweet that
          smells,
      If not from my love's breath? The purple pride,
      Which on thy soft cheek for complexion dwells,
5   In my love's veins thou hast too grossly dyed.'
      The lily I condemnèd for thy hand,
      And buds of marjoram had stol'n thy hair.
      The roses fearfully on thorns did stand,
      One blushing shame, another white despair,
10   A third nor red, nor white, had stol'n of both,
      And to his robb'ry had annexed thy breath;
      But for his theft, in pride of all his growth,
      A vengeful canker eat him up to death.
        More flowers I noted, yet I none could see
15   But sweet or colour it had stol'n from thee.

100   Where art thou, Muse, that thou forget'st so long
      To speak of that which gives thee all thy might?
      Spend'st thou thy fury on some worthless song,
      Dark'ning thy pow'r to lend base subjects light?
5   Return, forgetful Muse, and straight redeem
      In gentle numbers time so idly spent.
      Sing to the ear that doth thy lays esteem,
      And gives thy pen both skill and argument.
      Rise, resty Muse, my love's sweet face survey,
10   If Time have any wrinkle graven there;
      If any, be a satire to decay,
      And make Time's spoils despisèd everywhere.
        Give my love fame faster than Time wastes life,
        So thou prevent'st his scythe and crookèd knife.

101 O truant Muse, what shall be thy amends
   For thy neglect of truth in beauty dyed?
   Both truth and beauty on my love depends:
   So dost thou too, and therein dignified.
 5 Make answer, Muse, wilt thou not haply say
   'Truth needs no colour with his colour fixed,
   Beauty no pencil beauty's truth to lay,
   But best is best if never intermixed'?
   Because he needs no praise, wilt thou be dumb?
10 Excuse not silence so, for't lies in thee
   To make him much outlive a gilded tomb,
   And to be praised of ages yet to be.
    Then do thy office, Muse, I teach thee how,
    To make him seem long hence, as he shows now.

102 My love is strengthened though more weak in
      seeming;
   I love not less, though less the show appear.
   That love is merchandized whose rich esteeming
   The owner's tongue doth publish everywhere.
 5 Our love was new, and then but in the spring,
   When I was wont to greet it with my lays,
   As Philomel in summer's front doth sing,
   And stops his pipe in growth of riper days:
   Not that the summer is less pleasant now
10 Than when her mournful hymns did hush the night,
   But that wild music burdens every bough,
   And sweets grown common lose their dear delight.
    Therefore, like her, I sometime hold my tongue,
    Because I would not dull you with my song.

103   Alack, what poverty my Muse brings forth,
        That having such a scope to show her pride
        The argument all bare is of more worth
        Than when it hath my added praise beside.
  5 O, blame me not if I no more can write!
        Look in your glass, and there appears a face
        That overgoes my blunt invention quite,
        Dulling my lines, and doing me disgrace.
        Were it not sinful then, striving to mend,
 10 To mar the subject that before was well?
        For to no other pass my verses tend
        Than of your graces and your gifts to tell.
           And more, much more, than in my verse can sit
           Your own glass shows you, when you look in it.

104   To me, fair friend, you never can be old,
        For as you were when first your eye I eyed,
        Such seems your beauty still. Three winters cold
        Have from the forests shook three summers' pride,
  5 Three beauteous springs to yellow autumn turned
        In process of the seasons have I seen,
        Three April perfumes in three hot Junes burned,
        Since first I saw you fresh, which yet are green.
        Ah yet doth beauty, like a dial hand,
 10 Steal from his figure, and no pace perceived;
        So your sweet hue, which methinks still doth stand,
        Hath motion, and mine eye may be deceived.
           For fear of which, hear this thou age unbred:
           Ere you were born was beauty's summer dead.

105 Let not my love be called idolatry,
Nor my belovèd as an idol show,
Since all alike my songs and praises be
To one, of one, still such, and ever so.
5 Kind is my love today, tomorrow kind,
Still constant in a wondrous excellence;
Therefore my verse, to constancy confined,
One thing expressing, leaves out difference.
'Fair, kind, and true' is all my argument,
10 'Fair, kind, and true' varying to other words;
And in this change is my invention spent,
Three themes in one, which wondrous scope affords.
    Fair, kind, and true have often lived alone,
    Which three till now never kept seat in one.

106 When in the chronicle of wasted time
I see descriptions of the fairest wights,
And beauty making beautiful old rhyme
In praise of ladies dead, and lovely knights;
5 Then in the blazon of sweet beauty's best,
Of hand, of foot, of lip, of eye, of brow,
I see their antique pen would have expressed
Even such a beauty as you master now.
So all their praises are but prophecies
10 Of this our time, all you prefiguring,
And, for they looked but with divining eyes,
They had not skill enough your worth to sing:
    For we, which now behold these present days,
    Have eyes to wonder, but lack tongues to praise.

107 Not mine own fears, nor the prophetic soul
      Of the wide world, dreaming on things to come,
      Can yet the lease of my true love control,
      Supposed as forfeit to a confined doom.
  5 The mortal moon hath her eclipse endured,
      And the sad augurs mock their own presage.
      Incertainties now crown themselves assured,
      And peace proclaims olives of endless age.
      Now with the drops of this most balmy time
 10 My love looks fresh, and death to me subscribes,
      Since, spite of him, I'll live in this poor rhyme,
      While he insults o'er dull and speechless tribes.
          And thou in this shalt find thy monument,
          When tyrants' crests and tombs of brass are
             spent.

108 What's in the brain that ink may character,
      Which hath not figured to thee my true spirit?
      What's new to speak, what now to register,
      That may express my love, or thy dear merit?
  5 Nothing, sweet boy; but yet, like prayers divine,
      I must each day say o'er the very same,
      Counting no old thing old, thou mine, I thine,
      Even as when first I hallowed thy fair name.
      So that eternal love in love's fresh case
 10 Weighs not the dust and injury of age,
      Nor gives to necessary wrinkles place,
      But makes antiquity for aye his page,
          Finding the first conceit of love there bred,
          Where time and outward form would show it
             dead.

109   O, never say that I was false of heart,
Though absence seemed my flame to qualify.
As easy might I from myself depart,
As from my soul which in thy breast doth lie:
5 That is my home of love; if I have ranged,
Like him that travels I return again,
Just to the time, not with the time exchanged,
So that myself bring water for my stain.
Never believe, though in my nature reigned
10 All frailties that besiege all kinds of blood,
That it could so preposterously be stained,
To leave for nothing all thy sum of good:
    For nothing this wide universe I call,
    Save thou, my rose; in it thou art my all.

110   Alas 'tis true, I have gone here and there,
And made myself a motley to the view,
Gored my own thoughts, sold cheap what is most
    dear,
Made old offences of affections new.
5 Most true it is that I have looked on truth
Askance and strangely; but, by all above,
Those blenches gave my heart another youth,
And worse essays proved thee my best of love.
Now all is done, have what shall have no end.
10 Mine appetite I never more will grind
On newer proof, to try an older friend,
A god in love, to whom I am confined.
    Then give me welcome, next my heaven the best,
    Even to thy pure and most most loving breast.

111   O, for my sake do you with Fortune chide,
       The guilty goddess of my harmful deeds,
       That did not better for my life provide
       Than public means which public manners breeds.
  5 Thence comes it that my name receives a brand,
       And almost thence my nature is subdued
       To what it works in, like the dyer's hand.
       Pity me then, and wish I were renewed,
       Whilst, like a willing patient, I will drink
 10 Potions of eisel 'gainst my strong infection.
       No bitterness that I will bitter think,
       Nor double penance to correct correction.
          Pity me then, dear friend, and, I assure ye,
          Even that your pity is enough to cure me.

112   Your love and pity doth th' impression fill
       Which vulgar scandal stamped upon my brow,
       For what care I who calls me well or ill,
       So you o'er-green my bad, my good allow?
  5 You are my all the world, and I must strive
       To know my shames and praises from your tongue.
       None else to me, nor I to none alive,
       That my steeled sense or changes right or wrong.
       In so profound abysm I throw all care
 10 Of other's voices, that my adder's sense
       To critic and to flatterer stoppèd are:
       Mark how with my neglect I do dispense.
          You are so strongly in my purpose bred
          That all the world besides me thinks y' are dead.

113　Since I left you, mine eye is in my mind,
　　　And that which governs me to go about
　　　Doth part his function, and is partly blind,
　　　Seems seeing, but effectually is out:
　5　For it no form delivers to the heart
　　　Of bird, of flower, or shape which it doth latch.
　　　Of his quick objects hath the mind no part,
　　　Nor his own vision holds what it doth catch:
　　　For if it see the rud'st or gentlest sight,
　10　The most sweet-favour or deformèd'st creature,
　　　The mountain, or the sea, the day, or night,
　　　The crow, or dove, it shapes them to your feature.
　　　　　Incapable of more, replete with you,
　　　　　My most true mind thus makes mine eye untrue.

114　Or whether doth my mind, being crowned with you,
　　　Drink up the monarch's plague this flattery,
　　　Or whether shall I say mine eye saith true,
　　　And that your love taught it this alchemy?
　5　To make of monsters, and things indigest,
　　　Such cherubins as your sweet self resemble,
　　　Creating every bad a perfect best
　　　As fast as objects to his beams assemble?
　　　O, 'tis the first, 'tis flatt'ry in my seeing,
　10　And my great mind most kingly drinks it up.
　　　Mine eye well knows what with his gust is 'greeing,
　　　And to his palate doth prepare the cup.
　　　　　If it be poisoned, 'tis the lesser sin,
　　　　　That mine eye loves it and doth first begin.

115   Those lines that I before have writ do lie,
       Even those that said I could not love you dearer,
       Yet then my judgement knew no reason why
       My most full flame should afterwards burn clearer.
5   But reckoning time, whose millioned accidents
       Creep in 'twixt vows, and change decrees of kings,
       Tan sacred beauty, blunt the sharp'st intents,
       Diverts strong minds to th' course of alt'ring things.
       Alas why, fearing of Time's tyranny,
10   Might I not then say 'Now I love you best',
       When I was certain o'er incertainty,
       Crowning the present, doubting of the rest?
          Love is a babe, then might I not say so,
          To give full growth to that which still doth grow.

116   Let me not to the marriage of true minds
       Admit impediments; love is not love
       Which alters when it alteration finds,
       Or bends with the remover to remove.
5   O no, it is an ever-fixèd mark,
       That looks on tempests and is never shaken;
       It is the star to every wandering barque,
       Whose worth's unknown, although his height be
          taken.
       Love's not Time's fool, though rosy lips and cheeks
10   Within his bending sickle's compass come.
       Love alters not with his brief hours and weeks,
       But bears it out even to the edge of doom.
          If this be error and upon me proved,
          I never writ, nor no man ever loved.

117   Accuse me thus, that I have scanted all
       Wherein I should your great deserts repay,
       Forgot upon your dearest love to call,
       Whereto all bonds do tie me day by day,
5   That I have frequent been with unknown minds,
       And given to time your own dear-purchased right,
       That I have hoisted sail to all the winds
       Which should transport me farthest from your sight.
       Book both my wilfulness and errors down,
10   And on just proof, surmise accumulate,
       Bring me within the level of your frown,
       But shoot not at me in your wakened hate,
          Since my appeal says I did strive to prove
          The constancy and virtue of your love.

118   Like as to make our appetites more keen
       With eager compounds we our palate urge,
       As to prevent our maladies unseen
       We sicken to shun sickness when we purge;
5   Even so, being full of your ne'er-cloying sweetness,
       To bitter sauces did I frame my feeding,
       And, sick of welfare, found a kind of meetness
       To be diseased ere that there was true needing.
       Thus policy in love, t' anticipate
10   The ills that were not, grew to faults assurèd,
       And brought to medicine a healthful state,
       Which, rank of goodness, would by ill be curèd.
          But thence I learn, and find the lesson true,
          Drugs poison him that so fell sick of you.

119   What potions have I drunk of siren tears,
        Distilled from limbecks foul as hell within,
        Applying fears to hopes, and hopes to fears,
        Still losing when I saw myself to win?
  5   What wretched errors hath my heart committed,
        Whilst it hath thought itself so blessèd never?
        How have mine eyes out of their spheres been fitted
        In the distraction of this madding fever?
        O benefit of ill, now I find true
 10   That better is by evil still made better,
        And ruined love, when it is built anew,
        Grows fairer than at first, more strong, far greater.
          So I return rebuked to my content,
          And gain by ills thrice more than I have spent.

120   That you were once unkind befriends me now,
        And for that sorrow, which I then did feel,
        Needs must I under my transgression bow,
        Unless my nerves were brass or hammered steel.
  5   For if you were by my unkindness shaken,
        As I by yours, y' have passed a hell of time,
        And I, a tyrant, have no leisure taken
        To weigh how once I suffered in your crime.
        O that our night of woe might have rememb'red
 10   My deepest sense how hard true sorrow hits,
        And soon to you, as you to me then, tend'red
        The humble salve, which wounded bosom fits!
          But that your trespass now becomes a fee;
          Mine ransoms yours, and yours must ransom me.

121   'Tis better to be vile than vile esteemèd,
      When not to be receives reproach of being,
      And the just pleasure lost which is so deemèd
      Not by our feeling, but by others' seeing.
5   For why should others' false adulterate eyes
      Give salutation to my sportive blood?
      Or on my frailties why are frailer spies,
      Which in their wills count bad what I think good?
      No, I am that I am, and they that level
10 At my abuses reckon up their own;
      I may be straight though they themselves be bevel.
      By their rank thoughts my deeds must not be shown,
         Unless this general evil they maintain:
         All men are bad and in their badness reign.

122   Thy gift, thy tables, are within my brain
      Full charactered with lasting memory,
      Which shall above that idle rank remain
      Beyond all date even to eternity;
5   Or at the least so long as brain and heart
      Have faculty by nature to subsist,
      Till each to razed oblivion yield his part
      Of thee, thy record never can be missed.
      That poor retention could not so much hold,
10 Nor need I tallies thy dear love to score,
      Therefore to give them from me was I bold
      To trust those tables that receive thee more.
         To keep an adjunct to remember thee
         Were to import forgetfulness in me.

123 No! Time, thou shalt not boast that I do change.
       Thy pyramids built up with newer might
       To me are nothing novel, nothing strange;
       They are but dressings of a former sight.
   5 Our dates are brief, and therefore we admire
       What thou dost foist upon us that is old,
       And rather make them born to our desire
       Than think that we before have heard them told.
       Thy registers and thee I both defy,
 10 Not wond'ring at the present, nor the past,
       For thy records, and what we see, doth lie,
       Made more or less by thy continual haste.
         This I do vow and this shall ever be:
         I will be true despite thy scythe and thee.

124 If my dear love were but the child of state
       It might for Fortune's bastard be unfathered,
       As subject to Time's love, or to Time's hate,
       Weeds among weeds, or flowers with flowers
           gathered.
   5 No, it was builded far from accident,
       It suffers not in smiling pomp, nor falls
       Under the blow of thrallèd discontent,
       Whereto th' inviting time our fashion calls.
       It fears not policy, that heretic,
 10 Which works on leases of short-numb'red hours,
       But all alone stands hugely politic,
       That it nor grows with heat, nor drowns with
           show'rs.
         To this I witness call the fools of Time,
         Which die for goodness, who have lived for crime.

125 Were't aught to me I bore the canopy,
     With my extern the outward honouring,
     Or laid great bases for eternity,
     Which proves more short than waste or ruining?
5   Have I not seen dwellers on form and favour
     Lose all and more by paying too much rent,
     For compound sweet forgoing simple savour,
     Pitiful thrivers in their gazing spent?
     No, let me be obsequious in thy heart,
10 And take thou my oblation, poor but free,
     Which is not mixed with seconds, knows no art,
     But mutual render, only me for thee.
       Hence, thou suborned informer: a true soul
       When most impeached, stands least in thy control.

126 O thou my lovely boy, who in thy power
     Dost hold Time's fickle glass, his sickle hour;
     Who hast by waning grown, and therein show'st
     Thy lovers withering as thy sweet self grow'st –
5   If Nature (sovereign mistress over wrack)
     As thou goest onwards still will pluck thee back,
     She keeps thee to this purpose, that her skill
     May Time disgrace, and wretched minutes kill.
     Yet fear her, O thou minion of her pleasure:
10 She may detain, but not still keep, her treasure!
     Her audit (though delayed) answered must be,
     And her quietus is to render thee.
       (   )
       (   )

127 In the old age black was not counted fair,
Or if it were it bore not beauty's name;
But now is black beauty's successive heir,
And beauty slandered with a bastard shame:
5 For since each hand hath put on Nature's power,
Fairing the foul with Art's false borrowed face,
Sweet beauty hath no name, no holy bower,
But is profaned, if not lives in disgrace.
Therefore my mistress' eyes are raven black,
10 Her brows so suited, and they mourners seem
At such who, not born fair, no beauty lack,
Sland'ring creation with a false esteem.
  Yet so they mourn, becoming of their woe,
  That every tongue says beauty should look so.

128 How oft, when thou, my music, music play'st
Upon that blessèd wood whose motion sounds
With thy sweet fingers when thou gently sway'st
The wiry concord that mine ear confounds,
5 Do I envy those jacks that nimble leap
To kiss the tender inward of thy hand,
Whilst my poor lips, which should that harvest reap,
At the wood's boldness by thee blushing stand.
To be so tickled they would change their state
10 And situation with those dancing chips,
O'er whom thy fingers walk with gentle gait,
Making dead wood more blest than living lips.
  Since saucy jacks so happy are in this,
  Give them thy fingers, me thy lips to kiss.

129   Th' expense of spirit in a waste of shame
       Is lust in action, and, till action, lust
       Is perjured, murd'rous, bloody, full of blame,
       Savage, extreme, rude, cruel, not to trust,
5   Enjoyed no sooner but despisèd straight,
       Past reason hunted, and, no sooner had,
       Past reason hated as a swallowed bait
       On purpose laid to make the taker mad,
       Mad in pursuit, and in possession so,
10   Had, having, and in quest to have, extreme,
       A bliss in proof and proved a very woe,
       Before, a joy proposed; behind, a dream.
          All this the world well knows, yet none knows well
          To shun the heaven that leads men to this hell.

130   My mistress' eyes are nothing like the sun,
       Coral is far more red than her lips' red;
       If snow be white, why then her breasts are dun;
       If hairs be wires, black wires grow on her head.
5   I have seen roses damasked, red and white,
       But no such roses see I in her cheeks,
       And in some perfumes is there more delight
       Than in the breath that from my mistress reeks.
       I love to hear her speak, yet well I know
10   That music hath a far more pleasing sound.
       I grant I never saw a goddess go:
       My mistress when she walks treads on the ground.
          And yet, by heaven, I think my love as rare
          As any she belied with false compare.

131 Thou art as tyrannous, so as thou art,
     As those whose beauties proudly make them cruel,
     For well thou know'st to my dear doting heart
     Thou art the fairest and most precious jewel.
  5 Yet in good faith some say, that thee behold,
     Thy face hath not the power to make love groan;
     To say they err I dare not be so bold,
     Although I swear it to myself alone.
     And to be sure that is not false I swear
 10 A thousand groans but thinking on thy face
     One on another's neck do witness bear
     Thy black is fairest in my judgement's place.
         In nothing art thou black save in thy deeds,
         And thence this slander as I think proceeds.

132 Thine eyes I love, and they, as pitying me,
     Knowing thy heart torment me with disdain,
     Have put on black, and loving mourners be,
     Looking with pretty ruth upon my pain.
  5 And truly not the morning sun of heaven
     Better becomes the grey cheeks of the east,
     Nor that full star that ushers in the even
     Doth half that glory to the sober west
     As those two mourning eyes become thy face.
 10 O, let it then as well beseem thy heart
     To mourn for me, since mourning doth thee grace,
     And suit thy pity like in every part.
         Then will I swear beauty herself is black,
         And all they foul that thy complexion lack.

133 Beshrew that heart that makes my heart to groan
    For that deep wound it gives my friend and me.
    Is 't not enough to torture me alone,
    But slave to slavery my sweet'st friend must be?
  5 Me from myself thy cruel eye hath taken,
    And my next self thou harder hast engrossèd.
    Of him, myself, and thee I am forsaken,
    A torment thrice threefold thus to be crossèd.
    Prison my heart in thy steel bosom's ward,
 10 But then my friend's heart let my poor heart bail,
    Whoe'er keeps me, let my heart be his guard;
    Thou canst not then use rigour in my jail.
      And yet thou wilt, for I, being pent in thee,
      Perforce am thine, and all that is in me.

134 So now I have confessed that he is thine,
    And I myself am mortgaged to thy will;
    Myself I'll forfeit, so that other mine
    Thou wilt restore to be my comfort still.
  5 But thou wilt not, nor he will not be free,
    For thou art covetous, and he is kind.
    He learned but surety-like to write for me,
    Under that bond that him as fast doth bind.
    The statute of thy beauty thou wilt take,
 10 Thou usurer that put'st forth all to use,
    And sue a friend came debtor for my sake:
    So him I lose through my unkind abuse.
      Him have I lost, thou hast both him and me;
      He pays the whole, and yet I am not free.

135   Whoever hath her wish, thou hast thy Will,
      And Will to boot, and Will in overplus;
      More than enough am I that vex thee still,
      To thy sweet will making addition thus.
  5   Wilt thou, whose will is large and spacious,
      Not once vouchsafe to hide my will in thine?
      Shall will in others seem right gracious,
      And in my will no fair acceptance shine?
      The sea, all water, yet receives rain still,
 10 And in abundance addeth to his store;
      So thou, being rich in Will, add to thy Will
      One will of mine to make thy large Will more.
        Let 'no' unkind no fair beseechers kill:
        Think all but one, and me in that one Will.

136   If thy soul check thee that I come so near,
      Swear to thy blind soul that I was thy Will,
      And will, thy soul knows, is admitted there:
      Thus far for love my love-suit sweet fulfil.
  5   Will will fulfil the treasure of thy love,
      Ay, fill it full with wills, and my will one.
      In things of great receipt with ease we prove
      Among a number one is reckoned none;
      Then in the number let me pass untold,
 10 Though in thy store's account I one must be;
      For nothing hold me, so it please thee hold
      That nothing me, a something sweet to thee.
        Make but my name thy love, and love that still,
        And then thou lov'st me for my name is Will.

137   Thou blind fool love, what dost thou to mine eyes
      That they behold and see not what they see?
      They know what beauty is, see where it lies,
      Yet what the best is, take the worst to be.
5   If eyes corrupt by over-partial looks
      Be anchored in the bay where all men ride,
      Why of eyes' falsehood hast thou forgèd hooks,
      Whereto the judgement of my heart is tied?
      Why should my heart think that a several plot,
10   Which my heart knows the wide world's common
          place?
      Or mine eyes seeing this, say this is not,
      To put fair truth upon so foul a face?
        In things right true my heart and eyes have erred,
        And to this false plague are they now transferred.

138   When my love swears that she is made of truth,
      I do believe her though I know she lies,
      That she might think me some untutored youth,
      Unlearnèd in the world's false subtleties.
5   Thus vainly thinking that she thinks me young,
      Although she knows my days are past the best,
      Simply I credit her false-speaking tongue.
      On both sides thus is simple truth suppressed:
      But wherefore says she not she is unjust?
10   And wherefore say not I that I am old?
      O, love's best habit is in seeming trust,
      And age in love loves not to have years told.
        Therefore I lie with her, and she with me,
        And in our faults by lies we flattered be.

139 O call not me to justify the wrong
That thy unkindness lays upon my heart:
Wound me not with thine eye but with thy tongue,
Use power with power, and slay me not by art.
5 Tell me thou lov'st elsewhere; but in my sight,
Dear heart, forbear to glance thine eye aside.
What need'st thou wound with cunning when thy
      might
Is more than my o'erpressed defence can bide?
Let me excuse thee: 'Ah, my love well knows
10 Her pretty looks have been mine enemies,
And therefore from my face she turns my foes,
That they elsewhere might dart their injuries.'
    Yet do not so, but since I am near slain,
    Kill me outright with looks, and rid my pain.

140 Be wise as thou art cruel; do not press
My tongue-tied patience with too much disdain,
Lest sorrow lend me words, and words express
The manner of my pity-wanting pain.
5 If I might teach thee wit, better it were,
Though not to love, yet, love, to tell me so,
As testy sick men, when their deaths be near,
No news but health from their physicians know.
For if I should despair I should grow mad,
10 And in my madness might speak ill of thee.
Now this ill-wresting world is grown so bad,
Mad slanderers by mad ears believèd be.
    That I may not be so, nor thou belied,
    Bear thine eyes straight, though thy proud heart
      go wide.

141   In faith I do not love thee with mine eyes,
     For they in thee a thousand errors note,
     But 'tis my heart that loves what they despise,
     Who in despite of view is pleased to dote.
5   Nor are mine ears with thy tongue's tune delighted,
     Nor tender feeling to base touches prone,
     Nor taste, nor smell, desire to be invited
     To any sensual feast with thee alone;
     But my five wits nor my five senses can
10   Dissuade one foolish heart from serving thee,
     Who leaves unswayed the likeness of a man,
     Thy proud heart's slave and vassal wretch to be.
        Only my plague thus far I count my gain:
        That she that makes me sin awards me pain.

142   Love is my sin, and thy dear virtue hate,
     Hate of my sin, grounded on sinful loving.
     O, but with mine compare thou thine own state,
     And thou shalt find it merits not reproving,
5   Or if it do, not from those lips of thine
     That have profaned their scarlet ornaments
     And sealed false bonds of love as oft as mine,
     Robbed others' beds' revenues of their rents.
     Be it lawful I love thee as thou lov'st those,
10   Whom thine eyes woo as mine importune thee.
     Root pity in thy heart, that, when it grows
     Thy pity may deserve to pitied be.
        If thou dost seek to have what thou dost hide,
        By self example mayst thou be denied.

143 Lo, as a careful housewife runs to catch
One of her feathered creatures broke away,
Sets down her babe and makes all swift dispatch
In pursuit of the thing she would have stay,
5   Whilst her neglected child holds her in chase,
Cries to catch her whose busy care is bent
To follow that which flies before her face,
Not prizing her poor infant's discontent;
So runn'st thou after that which flies from thee,
10   Whilst I, thy babe, chase thee afar behind.
But if thou catch thy hope, turn back to me
And play the mother's part: kiss me, be kind.
   So will I pray that thou mayst have thy Will,
   If thou turn back and my loud crying still.

144 Two loves I have, of comfort and despair,
Which like two spirits do suggest me still.
The better angel is a man right fair;
The worser spirit a woman coloured ill.
5   To win me soon to hell my female evil
Tempteth my better angel from my side,
And would corrupt my saint to be a devil,
Wooing his purity with her foul pride.
And whether that my angel be turned fiend
10   Suspect I may, yet not directly tell,
But being both from me, both to each friend,
I guess one angel in another's hell.
   Yet this shall I ne'er know, but live in doubt,
   Till my bad angel fire my good one out.

145 Those lips that love's own hand did make
    Breathed forth the sound that said 'I hate'
    To me that languished for her sake;
    But when she saw my woeful state,
  5 Straight in her heart did mercy come,
    Chiding that tongue, that ever sweet
    Was used in giving gentle doom,
    And taught it thus anew to greet:
    'I hate' she altered with an end
10 That followed it as gentle day
    Doth follow night, who, like a fiend,
    From heaven to hell is flown away.
      'I hate' from hate away she threw
      And saved my life, saying 'not you.'

146 Poor soul, the centre of my sinful earth,
    Spoiled by these rebel powers that thee array,
    Why dost thou pine within and suffer dearth,
    Painting thy outward walls so costly gay?
  5 Why so large cost, having so short a lease,
    Dost thou upon thy fading mansion spend?
    Shall worms, inheritors of this excess,
    Eat up thy charge? Is this thy body's end?
    Then, soul, live thou upon thy servant's loss,
10 And let that pine to aggravate thy store;
    Buy terms divine in selling hours of dross;
    Within be fed, without be rich no more.
      So shall thou feed on Death, that feeds on men,
      And Death once dead, there's no more dying
        then.

147 My love is as a fever, longing still
For that which longer nurseth the disease,
Feeding on that which doth preserve the ill,
Th' uncertain sickly appetite to please.
5 My reason, the physician to my love,
Angry that his prescriptions are not kept,
Hath left me, and I desperate now approve
Desire is death, which physic did except.
Past cure I am, now Reason is past care,
10 And, frantic-mad with evermore unrest,
My thoughts and my discourse as madmen's are,
At random from the truth vainly expressed.
    For I have sworn thee fair, and thought thee bright,
    Who art as black as hell, as dark as night.

148 O me! What eyes hath love put in my head,
Which have no correspondence with true sight,
Or if they have, where is my judgement fled
That censures falsely what they see aright?
5 If that be fair whereon my false eyes dote
What means the world to say it is not so?
If it be not, then love doth well denote
Love's eye is not so true as all men's: no,
How can it? O, how can love's eye be true
10 That is so vexed with watching and with tears?
No marvel then though I mistake my view:
The sun itself sees not till heaven clears.
    O cunning love, with tears thou keep'st me blind,
    Lest eyes well-seeing thy foul faults should find.

149   Canst thou, O cruel, say I love thee not
      When I against myself with thee partake?
      Do I not think on thee when I forgot
      Am of myself, all tyrant for thy sake?
  5   Who hateth thee that I do call my friend?
      On whom frown'st thou that I do fawn upon?
      Nay, if thou lour'st on me do I not spend
      Revenge upon myself with present moan?
      What merit do I in myself respect
 10 That is so proud thy service to despise,
      When all my best doth worship thy defect,
      Commanded by the motion of thine eyes?
         But, love, hate on, for now I know thy mind:
         Those that can see, thou lov'st, and I am blind.

150   O, from what power hast thou this powerful might
      With insufficiency my heart to sway,
      To make me give the lie to my true sight,
      And swear that brightness doth not grace the day?
  5   Whence hast thou this becoming of things ill,
      That in the very refuse of thy deeds
      There is such strength and warrantize of skill
      That in my mind thy worst all best exceeds?
      Who taught thee how to make me love thee more,
 10 The more I hear and see just cause of hate?
      O, though I love what others do abhor,
      With others thou shouldst not abhor my state.
         If thy unworthiness raised love in me,
         More worthy I to be beloved of thee.

151   Love is too young to know what conscience is,
       Yet who knows not conscience is born of love?
       Then, gentle cheater, urge not my amiss,
       Lest guilty of my faults thy sweet self prove.
5   For thou betraying me, I do betray
       My nobler part to my gross body's treason.
       My soul doth tell my body that he may
       Triumph in love; flesh stays no farther reason,
       But, rising at thy name, doth point out thee
10 As his triumphant prize. Proud of this pride,
       He is contented thy poor drudge to be,
       To stand in thy affairs, fall by thy side.
          No want of conscience hold it that I call
          Her 'love', for whose dear love I rise and fall.

152   In loving thee thou know'st I am forsworn,
       But thou art twice forsworn, to me love swearing:
       In act thy bed-vow broke, and new faith torn
       In vowing new hate after new love bearing.
5   But why of two oaths' breach do I accuse thee,
       When I break twenty? I am perjured most,
       For all my vows are oaths but to misuse thee,
       And all my honest faith in thee is lost.
       For I have sworn deep oaths of thy deep kindness,
10 Oaths of thy love, thy truth, thy constancy,
       And to enlighten thee gave eyes to blindness,
       Or made them swear against the thing they see.
          For I have sworn thee fair: more perjured eye,
          To swear against the truth so foul a lie.

153   Cupid laid by his brand and fell asleep.
       A maid of Dian's this advantage found,
       And his love-kindling fire did quickly steep
       In a cold valley-fountain of that ground,
  5   Which borrowed from this holy fire of love
       A dateless lively heat, still to endure,
       And grew a seething bath, which yet men prove
       Against strange maladies a sovereign cure.
       But at my mistress' eye love's brand new fired,
 10   The boy for trial needs would touch my breast.
       I, sick withal, the help of bath desired,
       And thither hied, a sad distempered guest,
          But found no cure; the bath for my help lies
          Where Cupid got new fire: my mistress' eyes.

154   The little Love-god lying once asleep
       Laid by his side his heart-inflaming brand,
       Whilst many nymphs, that vowed chaste life to keep,
       Came tripping by; but in her maiden hand
  5   The fairest votary took up that fire,
       Which many legions of true hearts had warmed,
       And so the general of hot desire
       Was, sleeping, by a virgin hand disarmed.
       This brand she quenchèd in a cool well by,
 10   Which from love's fire took heat perpetual,
       Growing a bath and healthful remedy
       For men diseased; but I, my mistress' thrall,
          Came there for cure, and this by that I prove:
          Love's fire heats water; water cools not love.

Notes

Sonnets 1–126 are Petrarchan in style, although the poet is eulogizing a young male friend, rather than a distant and unattainable woman. Sonnets 1–17 urge the poet's 'master mistress' to marry and procreate; this would extend his family line and reproduce his beauty. Unfortunately, it soon becomes apparent that the youth is dedicated only to self-love.

1

1 **creatures** living things.
2 **That** so that.
  beauty's rose perhaps the symbol of female beauty. The 1609 quarto edition of the sonnets capitalized and italicized the word 'beauty', suggesting the Platonic ideal of the concept.
3 **But** so that, rather than 'contrary to expectation'.
  riper older.
4 **His** the possessive pronoun, 'his', signifies that the addressee is male.
  tender young, affectionate and sensitive.
5 **contracted** betrothed, but with the added meaning of being tied to a narcissistic love (self-love) of his *own bright eyes*. The notion is that the young man nourishes his ego with self-love; but, like a burning candle, he consumes himself with the flame.
7–8 The opposing ideas of *famine* and *abundance*, and *foe* and *sweet*, further sustain the idea that such a narcissistic attitude is self-destructive.
9 **fresh** youthful.
10 In this way, the youth is uniquely able to announce (*herald*) the rich and joyful (*gaudy*) season of spring.
11 As a *bud*, the youth is full of promise, but his life will be diminished as he buries all hopes of happiness and children.
  buriest to be read as two syllables.
12 The phrase *tender churl* echoes line 4 but, by placing apparently contradictory terms together (in an oxymoron), reinforces what

the rest of the line tells us: that the addressee *mak'st waste*, like
a 'niggard' (a miser) of his potentially fruitful youth. *mak'st
waste in niggarding* is a paradox, as it suggests that the young
man demonstrates wastefulness by hoarding.

13 **glutton** a greedy person. The sonnet continues to play with
the paradoxical notion that the youth greedily denies loving
another, and thereby procreating, in favour of self-love.

14 **the world's due** the young man's offspring, considered to be
his debt to the world.
by the grave and thee the young man will be devoured twice
over: both by himself and ultimately by death.

2

1 **forty winters** many; the chill of winter suggests the
destructive nature of time.

2 The natural images reinforce time's ravaging and blighting
effects, as wrinkles (*deep trenches*) are dug into the youth's once-
beautiful image (*beauty's field*).

3 **proud livery** splendid – and perhaps arrogant – appearance.
livery, as 'uniform', also suggests that the youth's appearance is
not permanent.

4 **tattered weed** means both (1) torn garment and (2) an
uncultivated plant; the second meaning continues the
metaphors of nature that began in line 2.

6 **treasure** the image of the youth hoarding his beauty is played
out against the allusion to the parable of the talents (Matthew
25:14–30), where God is a lord who presents his servants with
money to spend, not to save.

7 **deep-sunken eyes** a contrast to Sonnet 1:5, where the eyes in
youth are *bright*. There is also a clear pun on the word 'eye'
with 'I' – feeding the image of the young man burying future
selves within himself.

8 **all-eating shame** this recalls both the reference to gluttony, at
the end of Sonnet 1 and the notion that allowing time to
devour everything is unprofitable (*thriftless*), self-destructive and
shameful.

11 **sum my count** to add up the assets of life.
    make my old excuse to justify, and make valuable, the life that the youth has lived.

12 **Proving** demonstrating (as a result of the likeness of the offspring).
    by succession (fairness that comes by) right of inheritance.

13–14 When the young man grows old, he will see the beauty and hot-bloodedness of youth, as well as his blood-line, renewed in the figure of his child.

3

1–2 These lines command the youth to view his reflected face, to remind him to replicate it.

3 **fresh repair** good condition.

4 **beguile** deceive; trick.
    unbless some mother to refuse to bless a potential mother with offspring.

5 **uneared** untilled, thereby not producing fruit; here, the image of procreation is described, metaphorically, in terms of agriculture.

6 **husbandry** (1) farming and (2) performing the duties of a husband.

7 **fond** (1) foolish and (2) selfishly narcissistic.
    tomb the youth's own body, as he selfishly buries all chances of posterity.

9 **glass** a mirror image; as the mother's youth is reflected in her son, so will the young man's be reflected in his offspring.

10 **lovely April** youth, coming from the proverb, 'In the April of one's age'.

11 **windows of thine age** metaphor for aged eyes.

12 **Despite of wrinkles** in spite of the wrinkles the youth will one day have.
    golden time youth; the young man will be enabled to play out his youth through his child.

13 **rememb'red not to be** desiring not to be remembered.

14 **image** (1) a mirror image (line 1), (2) a child, and (3) a mental image or memory.

4

1 **Unthrifty** wasted and profitless, echoing Sonnet 2:8.
spend pre-empts the metaphor of beauty being inherited for
the purpose of spending.
2 **beauty's legacy** (1) the beauty that the youth has inherited and
(2) the beauty that he must, in turn, bequeath to his children.
3 **but doth lend** Nature lends youth and beauty, expecting a
return (i.e. offspring) on her loan.
4 **frank** generous.
5 **beauteous niggard** beautiful miser, with *beauteous* to be read
as two syllables. An oxymoron (apparent contradiction in
terms), suggesting that the youth fails to be generous with what
Nature has given him.
6 **bounteous largess** the liberal gift (of youth and beauty).
7 **Profitless usurer** usurers lend money at an incredibly high
rate of interest. This phrase is an oxymoron.
use spend or make use of.
8 **sum of sums** grand total.
live make a living.
9 **having traffic with** (1) trading with and (2) being sexually
interested in.
10 **of thyself** due to the youth's own actions.
12 **acceptable audit** final reckoning.
13 **unused** continuing the image of youth and beauty being used
for profit, this word brands the young man as a wastrel.
14 **th' executor** legal agent; in this case, the child, who would
'execute' his father's beauty into the future.

5

1 **hours** to be read as a disyllable.
gentle work the mild and moderate working of time, which
serves to create the beauty of the young man.
frame make.
2 **gaze** the youth as the object of the gaze, as all eyes fall upon
him.

3 **same**   refers to *lovely gaze*, line 2.

4 Time, that so *fairly* framed the youth, will make him not-fair in its same careful destruction of his beauty; the pun on 'fair' emphasizes this point.

5 **leads summer on**   (1) guides and (2) charms.

6 **hideous**   dreadful.
 confounds   destroys.

7 **checked**   stopped.
 lusty   vigorous.

8 **Beauty o'er-snowed**   the greenness of nature covered with snow, acts as a metaphor for the whiteness of human hair in old age.
 bareness everywhere   paradox, putting the emphasis upon bleakness and isolation. It is interesting to note that the 1609 quarto edition's spelling, *barenes*, was a seventeenth-century spelling for 'barrenness'.

9 **summer's distillation**   relating to beauty's rose (Sonnet 1:2), this refers to rose-water.

10 This line suggests that the essence of summer/youth – rose-water – be confined to a glass vial. Shakespeare would have known Philip Sidney's *Arcadia* (1590) well: 'Have you ever seen a pure rose-water kept in a crystal glass, how fine it looks, how sweet it smells while that beautiful glass imprisons it? Break the prison, and let the water take its own course; doth it not embrace dust and lose all his former sweetness and fairness? Truly so are we, if we have not the stay, rather than the restraint, of crystalline marriage.' Here, Shakespeare suggests that longevity is attained, not through marriage, but through children.

11–12 The essence, and impact, of beauty would be lost – as would be all memory of it.

13 **flowers distilled**   the perfume of flowers preserved in water.

14 **substance**   essence.

6

1 **Then let not**   this sonnet is a direct continuation of Sonnet 5.
 ragged   rough.
 deface   destroy.

2 **distilled**   preserved by having children.

3 **vial**   a metaphor for the womb.

5 **use**   usury (money lending) was legalized in 1571 and the notion of it is, here, applied to intercourse. Both usury and intercourse are acceptable if profitable.

6 **happies**   produces happiness.

7 **breed**   referring to both a usurer's money and begetting offspring.

8–9 **ten for one**   the legalized usurer's interest rate was ten per cent; should the youth multiply himself tenfold, he would be ten times more content.

10–12 The notion of lineage continues, with the youth's offspring bearing one hundred grandchildren for posterity.

13 **self-willed**   is reminiscent of *self-killed* in line 4. The pun on 'will' relates to (1) wilful, (2) bequeathing goods only to himself, and (3) being concerned only with his own sexual desire.

fair   both beautiful and equitable.

14 Death will conquer the youth's body, such that his decaying body will feed the worms. A secondary meaning hints at the notion of conquest in terms of property being acquired without inheritance.

7

1 **gracious light**   the monarchical sun.

2 **each under-eye**   each eye observing from below.

3 **new appearing sight**   dawn.

4 **Serving with looks**   casting down their eyes, as they bow.

5 **And having climbed**   the sun reaches its zenith at noon.

6 **middle age**   represents the prime of life, as in Aristotle's *Rhetoric* (fourth century BC: Sonnet 2:12–14).

7 **still**   his beauty is unmoving, fixed.

8 **Attending on**   waiting on, as courtiers did upon the monarch.

9 **highmost pitch**   zenith.

weary car   a metonym (closely associated substitute) for the weary sun, 'car' signifying 'chariot'.

10 **reeleth**   the sun begins to set.

11 **fore** formerly: the message being that the eyes worship the sun forenoon.

    converted turned away.

12 **tract** track.

13 As the sun, at its zenith, is about to fall, so too the youth, in his prime, is teetering upon the brink of decline.

14 **get a son** a pun on the word 'sun', suggesting that the youth beget a male heir before it is too late.

8

1 **Music to hear** the poet suggests that the youth's voice is like music to his ears.

    sadly gravely.

2 **Sweets** things that bring delight.

4 **annoy** pain.

5 **true concord** harmony.

6 **By unions married** harmonious chords.

7 **sweetly chide** chastize with sweet notes.

    confounds destroys (the harmony).

8 **In singleness** in being single (unmarried), and by not blending his voice to the tune of others, the youth destroys the harmony.

    parts both the parts assigned in melody-making and those parts of the youth that ought to be passed on to future generations.

9–10 This could refer to single musical strings being played together in mutual harmony or to the tuning of an instrument such that each string has the same tension as the next. In either case, the meaning is a metaphor for marriage, with *strikes* signifying sexual intercourse.

13 **speechless** wordless.

14 **Thou single wilt prove none** alluding to the proverb that 'one' is no number, the youth is warned that his ancestral line will die out should he remain a bachelor.

9

1 **widow**   his prospective wife, left to weep after the youth's death.
2 **consum'st**   waste.
3 **issueless**   without offspring.
   hap   chance.
4 **makeless**   without a mate.
5 **still**   constantly. Note also the alliterative 'w', which adds dramatic force to this line.
6 **form**   likeness.
7 **private**   individual.
8 **By children's eyes**   by looking into the eyes of her children, the widow will recall the likeness of her dead husband.
9 **Look what**   whatever.
   unthrift   has parted with his wealth, but it remains in the world.
11 **beauty's waste**   beauty will be wasted, unless put to use in procreation. Beauty, that is *unused* by the user (the individual failing to use it), will be destroyed.
14 **murd'rous shame**   the youth commits a shameful act in refusing to perpetuate his family line; there is also the suggestion that shame may well be the death of him. There is also a secondary allusion to masturbation, and the commonly held Renaissance view that the man shortens his life with each orgasm.

10

1 **For shame**   continues the reference in Sonnet 9. Here, it means 'as a result of shame'.
2 **unprovident**   improvident.
3 **Grant, if thou wilt**   it may be argued, if the youth so wishes.
5 **possessed with murd'rous hate**   the youth is possessed, as if by demons, with a hate that builds upon the reference to shame in Sonnet 9:14.
6 **stick'st not**   does not hesitate.

7 **that beauteous roof** the youth seeks to ruin his own family, or house, by ruining any chance he has to procreate. As the roof of the house, he is its head, and so has the power to provide an heir.

8 **repair** keep the possibility of lineage and, therefore, posterity in good order.

9 If the youth should change his outlook, the poet would then think more highly of him.

10 **fairer lodged** have a more beautiful outer body.

11 Relating to the theory of physiognomy, where the outer body was believed to reflect the inner soul.

12 **kind-hearted** refers both to being amiable in nature, as well as to the love that should be shown to kindred.

13 Should the youth produce an heir, the poet would think much more highly of him.

14 An heir would ensure that the youth's beauty lived on: both in his offspring and himself.

11

1 **fast** speedily and steadily.

2 The young man's fast departing youth will be seen to grow in his offspring.

3 **fresh blood** signifies both semen, made all the stronger in the young man's youth and the blood that will be inherited by his children.

4 **convertest** move away from.

5 **Herein** if the youth should, indeed, marry and procreate.

6 **Without this** if the youth should remain a bachelor.

7 **minded** of the same mind as the youth.

8 the world would be without people within 60 years (*threescore year*).

9 **for store** for hoarding and preserving, a nature metaphor for rearing and nurturing children.

10 **Harsh, featureless, and rude** rough, ill-featured and uncouth. This image perhaps refers to the lower classes.

11 This line carries echoes of Mark 4:25: 'For he that hath, to him shall be given: and he that hath not, from him shall be taken even that which he hath.'

12 **in bounty cherish**   in use, the youth's bounty will increase.

13 **seal**   nature is said to make every individual in her own image. Only procreation can ensure that the seal is continued.

14 **print more**   produce more children.

12

1 **count the clock**   the passage of time is calculated by counting the chimes of the clock.

2 **brave**   splendid.

sunk   the image of the sun going down.

3 **prime**   (1) early morning, (2) spring, or (3) youth.

4 **sable**   black.

5 **barren**   (1) bare and (2) infertile.

6 **erst**   formerly.

canopy the herd   give shade to the cattle.

7 **summer's green**   a natural image, implying the freshness of youth.

girded up   the tying up of the sheaves of corn can also refer to the carrying of the dead into the church.

8 **bier**   a barrow for carrying the cut corn or a litter for transporting dead bodies. The comparison is due to the fact that, once harvested, the corn can no longer grow.

white and bristly beard   when the harvest is cut and dried, it turns white like an old man's beard. The metaphor is therefore extended.

9 **question make**   the poet questions the youth's beauty, since it will not last forever.

10 The youth will waste his time on earth, destined to become a ruin at the hands of time.

11 Those things on earth that were once sweet and beautiful will cease to be so.

12 Echoing Sonnet 11:1–2: as fast as a child grows to youth and beauty, so too does every individual waste and decay.

13 **And nothing**   literally, there will come a day when the youth will be unable to save his family line. Note that the word 'nothing' also referred to female genitalia, which will be unable to help him.

Time's scythe   both Time and Death were pictured with the scythe as a weapon.

14 Only children (*breed*) can save the youth from extinction.

13

This is the first time that the poet addresses the youth as 'you', rather than the more personal 'thou'.

1 The poet wishes that the youth were an essential self (soul) and thereby immortal.

2 However, the youth is subject to time, here in the real world.

3 **Against**   in guarding against.
this coming end   death.

4 **sweet semblance**   beautiful outward appearance, which carries notions of seeming due to its transience.

5 **hold in lease**   in the legal sense, hold in leasehold: again, the youth's beauty is not permanent.

6 **determination**   end.

7 **Yourself**   your essential self (soul).

9 **so fair a house**   a metaphor for the youth's beautiful body.

10 **husbandry**   (1) management of a household, with a pun on the idea of being a husband and (2) farming (see Sonnet 3:5–6).

11 **winter's day**   a metaphor for old age.

12 **barren rage**   the poet suggests that the youth's great anger and frustration, once he is dead, will be futile.

13 **unthrifts**   spendthrifts (see Sonnet 9:9).

14 The line suggests that the son is already in existence: to deny him a father would be to kill him.

14

1 **judgement pluck**   the poet does not take his knowledge from astronomy.

2 **I have astronomy**   he does understand astronomy.

4 **dearths**   famines.
seasons' quality   the nature of the seasons.

5 He cannot foretell the future.

6 He cannot predict what the weather will be.

7 **say with princes** predict the fortune of princes.

8 **in heaven find** read in the stars.

9 **thine eyes** the eyes were thought to be the windows of the soul.

10 **constant stars** the poet finds true divination in the youth's eyes, and not in the stars. The commonplace comparison of the eyes with the stars underlies this notion, although a woman's eyes were the conventional object.

11 **truth and beauty** once again, alluding to the theory of physiognomy, the poet wishes that the youth's soul (*truth*) would match his outer self (*beauty*).

12 Should the youth transform (*convert*) his current characteristics, and procreate, his own truth and beauty would provide resources for the future (*store*). This line echoes the sentiments expressed in Sonnet 13.

13 **prognosticate** forecast.

14 **doom and date** the youth's truth and beauty, without offspring, is bound to be limited in time and fated to die.

15

1 **consider every thing** consider that everything.

2 **Holds in perfection** (1) remains perfect and (2) stays at the point of perfection (i.e. its prime).

3 **huge stage presenteth nought but shows** this metaphor compares the world to a stage, whereupon all human actions are empty and false. See *As You Like It* (1599) 2:7:138–40:

4 It is the stars that look upon the world like an audience, witnessing human insincerity. They view in secret, as this is a mystical practice, and their criticism influences human behaviour; influence is the astrological term for the ethereal fluid or occult power seen to come from the stars, affecting a person's future actions.

5 **as plants increase** grow as plants do.

6 **Cheerèd and checked** encouraged and restrained.
selfsame sky the stars, that randomly deliver good and bad fortune.

7 **Vaunt** praise or herald.
 at height decrease at the pinnacle of youth, all human beings (and plants) must, of necessity, begin to decline and decay.
8 The *brave state* is beauty, which decays over time until even the memory of it is lost.
9 **conceit** thought; realization.
 inconstant stay impermanent time on earth (with echoes of the decline of the human form as it moves towards death).
10 **rich in youth** in the prime of life.
11 **Where** in the youth's sight.
 wasteful time debateth with decay (1) time and decay argue over (*debateth*) how they each might waste the human body, (2) time and decay argue over who should be the first to destroy youth, or (3) time enters into a fight (*debateth*) with the youth, armed with decay.
12 **sullied night** a metaphor to suggest that tarnished age follows youth, as night follows day.
13 **all in war** the poet is at war with Time.
14 The plant image is allowed to develop, this time building upon the notion of one plant being allowed to grow on another (engrafting). The poet metaphorically suggests that his own pen will engraft the youth into the future, if future generations do not.

16

1 **But** continuing the argument from Sonnet 15.
 a mightier way a more powerful way than by the aforementioned 'grafting'.
3 **fortify** strengthen.
4 The poet now sees his poems as woefully inadequate; only procreation will bear the necessary fruit.
5 **the top of happy hours** the youth is in his prime, at present.
6 **unset** unplanted; a metaphor for virginity.
7 **virtuous** the state of marriage would bring both chastity and sound morals.
 living flowers offspring.

8 **liker** more in the youth's image.
   painted counterfeit a painting or a poem.
9 **lines of life** (1) lineage, (2) features of the youth's offspring, and (3) lines drawn in painting or in writing a poem.
   that life repair restore.
10 **this time's pencil** the sonnets about the youth, written with a small brush (pencil), cannot completely bring the subject to life in all his perfection.
   pupil pen the poet modestly sees his early sonnets about the youth as being those of a novice.
11 **inward worth nor outward fair** the two aspects of beauty which, according to the theory of physiognomy, ought to match.
12 **yourself** both the inner and the outer youth.
   in eyes of men to the world.
13 The youth's sense of self will only be retained with the stability, and continuity, that marriage and children will bring.
14 Only by becoming his own painter or poet (i.e. by producing children) can the youth hope to conquer time.

17

This is the last of what have become known as the procreation sonnets.

2 **high deserts** both physical and spiritual goodness.
3 **a tomb** the poet insists that his verse can only act as a tomb, failing to display the youth's living essence (*your life*) and abilities (*parts*).
5 **write** express in verse.
6 And in metrical lines of verse (*numbers*) count up (*number*) all the youth's virtues (*graces*).
7 **age to come** in the future generation.
8 **heavenly touches** celestial strokes of the brush or pen.
9 **papers** verses.
10 **old men of less truth than tongue** a simile that suggests that the poems will lose their authority with age, just as old men lie

with age. The latter was a common proverb at the time: 'Old men and travellers may lie by authority'.

11 **true rights**   what the youth deserves, with a pun on 'rites'.
 a poet's rage   according to classical thinking, *furor poeticus* is the passionate state of mind of the composing poet.

12 **stretchèd metre**   perhaps alluding either to the hyperbolic style of many poems or to the overly long lines that affected the regularity of metre.
 antique song   an ancient song, with a pun on 'antic' (meaning grotesque).

13 **that time**   in the generation to follow.

14 **rhyme**   verse.

18

This sonnet introduces an additional argument, referring to the writing of poetry as a means of preserving the youth's beauty and virtuous qualities.

The focus now moves from having children, as the main method of preserving the youth's beauty, to art. The poet puts forward the argument that he can reproduce his friend's image in poetry.

2 **temperate**   moderate.

3 **May**   in the 1590s, the month of May was a little behind our modern European calendar. For this reason, May extended into our month of June, thus firmly making it a summer month.

4 The summer season is only temporary and so has a very short lease on nature.

5 **Sometime**   at times.
 eye of heaven   the sun.

6 **gold complexion**   the bright yellow face of the sun, extending the imagery from Sonnet 7:1–2.
 dimmed   obscured by clouds.

7 The sun becomes a metaphor for the human individual, whose fairness declines from its state of beauty to a state of gradual decline.

8 **chance**   (bad) luck.
  nature's changing course   natural decay.
  untrimmed   stripped.
10 **fair**   fairness.
  ow'st   (1) own and (2) as a debt, to be paid to Death.
11 **his shade**   a reference to Psalms 23:3: 'Yea, though I walk
  through the valley of the shadow of death, I will fear no evil:
  for thou art with me; thy rod and thy staff they comfort me.'
12 **eternal lines**   immortal verse.
14 **this**   this sonnet.
  life   immortality.

19

1 **Devouring Time**   Ovid's Latin phrase, *tempus edax rerum*
  (*Metamorphoses* 15:234) became loosely translated into the well-
  known sixteenth-century proverb, 'Time devours all things'.
  Note that the concept of time is personified.
2 The earth takes back into itself all human beings, once time has
  wasted them and they have died. G. Blakemore Evans (2006)
  asks us to remember the Book of Common Prayer, *earth to
  earth, ashes to ashes, dust to dust*, while alerting us to the fact that
  there is no mention of 'a future state' in this sonnet.
4 According to legend, the phoenix is an immortal bird, that
  lives for several hundred years before being burned on a pyre lit
  by the sun. It then is born anew from its own ashes, for the
  cycle to begin again (Ovid, *Amores*, 15:392–402). However,
  Shakespeare appears to dwell upon the phoenix's death, at the
  hands of time, rather than its powers of regeneration. This
  carries echoes of Shakespeare's epic poem *The Phoenix and the
  Turtle* (1601), where the phoenix is seen to die without heirs.
5 Time delivers seasons that are both fortunate and unfortunate,
  as in Ovid's four ages of man (*Metamorphoses* 15:199–213).
  With the reference to *fleet'st*, it becomes clear that time is now
  acting in a more speedy fashion.
6 **swift-footed**   a continuing image of the rapidity of time.
7 **sweets**   an allusion to earth's children (*sweet brood*) in line 2.

9 **carve not with thy hours** the poet asks time not to carve wrinkles into the face of the youth.

10 **no lines** the pun on 'lines' relates both to time's wrinkles and the poet's *eternal lines* (Sonnet 18:12).

11 **course** rapid progress of time; there may also be an allusion to hunting here, as the notion of horse racing came with *swift-footed* (line 6).
untainted unaffected and unsullied.

12 **pattern** the pattern of beauty; the ideal.

13 **Yet** the argument is turned around with the use of this word, meaning 'in spite of that'.

14 **My love** meaning (1) the youth himself and (2) the love that the poet feels.

20

1 **with nature's own hand** the youth has been blessed with an unadorned, natural beauty; unlike women, whose beauty comes from art.

2 **master mistress** (1) a reference to the unconventional nature of the poem, with the man being addressed in a way typical of a woman (if passion is to mean the sonnet itself) and (2) the notion that the man has the same sort of delicate, feminine beauty as a woman.

3–4 Despite having beauty and a woman's gentle heart, the youth is not fickle as women were thought to be.

5 **less false in rolling** although the youth's eyes do roll on occasion, they are less inclined to do so than a woman's eyes, which roll due to inconstancy.

6 **Gilding** surfacing with gold, as the sun does.

7 In the sixteenth century, hue meant 'form' or 'outward appearance', with an emphasis upon good looks, as well as 'colour', perhaps relating to complexion. The reference to *all hues* suggests that the youth's beauty has elements of both the male and the female, as he is able to control his own form; it can also refer to his ability to enthral both men and women with his looks, thereby controlling each of them.

9 **for a woman** as a woman.

10 Nature created the youth as a woman initially, until she fell in love with the image of her own making.

11 **by addition** by adding a penis.
   defeated deprived.

12 **to my purpose nothing** no use to a man, with a pun on the word 'nothing' (as in 'no thing' – a vagina).

13 **pricked thee out** Nature chose the youth, there being a pun on the word 'prick' (penis).

14 The poet wishes that the youth's spiritual love be with him, while his physical love can lead to marriage and posterity.

21

The poet rejects the elaborate metaphors of other poets, who aim to glorify their subjects; he prefers truth and sincerity.

1 **that Muse** a metonym (closely associated substitute) for the poet, who is inspired by the Muse.

2 **Stirred** inspired.
   painted beauty echoes the reference to women as painted beauties in Sonnet 22, painted both with cosmetics and with the hyperbole (exaggeration) of the poet's pen.

3 The poet may further beautify his beautiful female subject by comparing her with heaven, the latter perhaps being a (blasphemic) metonym for God.

4 He may then continue to compare (rehearse) his subject with every other beautiful thing on earth.

5 Such exalted similes will result in impressive couplings (*couplement*).

6 **gems** treasures of the earth and sea.

7 **April's** refers to the coming of spring.
   first-born in the quarto version, the spelling is *first-borne*, which suggests the first flowers that spring brings.
   rare beautiful, good and unusual.

8 **this huge rondure hems** the spherical universe is bounded.

9 **truly** the poet wishes to write sincerely, without the exaggerated comparisons that other poets use.

11 **any mother's child** the poet insists that he loves the youth as much as any mother loves her own child.
12 **those gold candles** the stars.
13 **say more** exaggerate.
   hearsay gossip.
14 Alludes to the proverb, 'He praises who wishes to sell', meaning that public compliment is vulgar and commercial.

22

1 **glass** mirror.
   old traditionally, the poet would allude to his mistress's youth in his verse and therefore his own age by comparison. Shakespeare would have been nearly 35 when he wrote this sonnet, which would have been viewed as middle aged, by today's standards.
2 **of one date** can live mutually together.
3 **time's furrows** wrinkles.
4 **look** anticipate.
   expiate atone for.
5 **cover** clothe.
6 **seemly** becoming.
9 **wary** cautious.
10 **will** the poet will also be cautious for the youth (with a pun, suggesting desire).
11 **chary** charily, carefully.
12 **tender** loving.
   faring ill (1) coming to any harm or (2) eating ill food.
13–14 **Presume not on** the final couplet implies that the youth will not recover his own heart, having misused the poet's so badly.

23

1 **an unperfect actor** an actor who does not learn his lines.
2 **with his fear** stage-fright.
   put besides forgets his lines.

3 **replete**   filled.
4 **heart**   passion or courage.
5 **for fear of trust**   the poet is unable to trust himself.
6 **perfect**   flawless.
   rite   a pun on this word suggests both ritual and a claim.
7 **decay**   weaken.
8 **O'er-charged**   encumbered.
9 **my books**   my writings.
10 **dumb presagers**   silent warnings.
11 **look for recompense**   search for love to be requited.
13 **silent love**   the sixteenth-century proverb, 'Whom we love best
   to them we can say least', may well inform this line; the
   implication is that the poet's love is so sincere that he finds it
   difficult to articulate it.
14 **fine wit**   intelligence.

24

1 **stelled**   fixed.
2 **form**   image.
   table   writing tablet.
3 **frame**   easel.
4 **perspective**   refers both to (1) the painter's ability to represent
   distance and (2) the 'perspective glass', an instrument used to
   magnify objects invisible to the human eye.
5 **through the painter**   only the painter's eye is truly able to see
   the perspective, thereby seeing into the youth's heart.
6 **true**   faithful.
7 **bosom's shop**   the heart.
8 Only the painter (or lover) can see the essence of the model (or
   beloved).
9 **good turns**   favours.
11–12 **wherethrough**   through which.
   the sun   the sun is also in love with the youth.
13–14 However, the eyes can only draw what they can see; they can
   never really know the heart.

25

1 **who are in favour with their stars** lucky.
3 **fortune of** position in society.
4 **Unlooked for** overlooked.
5 **fair** beautiful.
6 **marigold** seen to open and close with the sun.
7 **pride** favouritism comes only when a prince looks upon a subject, in the same way as when the sun looks upon the flower.
8 **frown** the displeasure of princes, imaged in the clouds that appear when the sun is out of sight.
9 **painful** painstaking.
   famousèd made famous.
10 **once foiled** once defeated.
11 **razèd** erased.
12 **toiled** fought.
13–14 This sonnet ends much more positively, as the poet insists upon the permanence of his love, unlike the fickle favours of fortune.

26

1 **vassalage** service.
2 **duty** willingness to serve.
3 **ambassage** message.
4 **witness** the poem itself will bear witness to the poet's love for the youth.
   wit intelligence.
5 **poor** lacking.
6 **seem bare** unadorned and empty.
7 **good conceit** kind act or imaginative impulse.
8 **soul's thought** inner emotions.
9 **moving** motion in life.
10 **Points on me** looks favourably upon the poet, as in astrological terms.
   fair aspect positive astrological influence.
11 **my tattered loving** the notion that the poet is unable to clothe his love in the verbal finery that his being deserves.

14 **not show my head** makes reference to the proverb about the debtor, 'He dares not show his head'; the poet will not allow himself to be put in a position where he must prove his love.

27

Sonnets 27 and 28 are on the subject of night and sleeplessness, a traditional motif in Petrarchan love poetry.

2 **dear repose** precious place to rest (bed).
  travail meaning both a journey and a toil.
3 **journey** picking up on the meaning of the previous line, an imaginary voyage or toil.
4 **work** make it work.
  expirèd has finished, meaning loss of breath.
5 **from far** his thoughts begin their arduous and long journey towards the youth's abode.
6 **Intend** start out on.
  pilgrimage the poet sees himself as a pilgrim lover, searching out the shrine of his true love.
8 **see** it is a paradox that the blind 'see' darkness.
9 **imaginary sight** the soul's imagination.
10 **shadow** image.
  sightless view see as a blind individual.
11 **like a jewel** some jewels were thought to cast light.
  ghastly horrifying.
12 This line is the first example of opposition, one of Shakespeare's favourite devices in his sonnets.
14 **For thee, and for myself** the youth inflicts pain upon the poet and the poet allows himself to feel the pain.
  no quiet find the poet can find no peace or solace.

28

1 **happy plight** a good and cheerful condition.
2 **debarred** forbidden.
3 **oppression** the aforementioned journey and toil (Sonnet 27:2).

    4 This line refers to the never-ending cycle of distress that love creates; day and night have entered into a pact to continually torment their subject.

7–8 The day will torture the poet through toil (the *day's oppression* (line 3)), while the night will cause him to grieve over the growing distance from the youth.

    9 In order to please the sun, the poet tells him that the youth is as bright as he.

  10 **grace** honour.

  11 **swart-complexioned** black or dark-skinned.

  12 **twire** peep.
       gild'st tinge with gold light.
       the even evening.

  13 **draw** draw out, lengthen.

  14 Night makes the poet's sorrow seem even longer.

29

    1 **disgrace** out of favour.

    2 **beweep** weep for.
       outcast state feeling of being outcast, by both (1) Fortune and (2) society.

    3 **trouble deaf heaven** annoy God, such that He turns a deaf ear.
       bootless hopeless.

    4 **Look upon myself** self-contemplate.

    5 **one more rich in hope** someone with more hope in life.

    6 **Featured like him** with the beautiful features of another.

    7 **art** skill and learning
       scope opportunity.

    8 **what I most enjoy** it is unclear as to what the poet most enjoys, but it may be his poetry.

  10 **Haply** perhaps, punning on the notion of 'happily'.

11–12 By thinking about the youth, the poet's sullen attitude is overtaken by the exalted state imaged by the lark singing at heaven's gate.

  13 **wealth** happiness.

  14 At that point, the poet would not exchange his state for a kingdom.

30

1 **sessions** court sittings.
2 **summon up** cause to appear.
3 **lack** want.
4 **dear time's waste** (1) a waste of the prime years of the poet's life and (2) a waste of what the poet holds dear to him.
5 **unused to flow** not used to crying.
6 **dateless** endless.
7 **cancelled** a legal term, referring to the woe that has been paid for.
8 **moan th' expense** bemoan the loss.
9 **grievances fore-gone** previous sorrows.
10 **heavily** sadly.
11 **sad account** (1) sad story and (2) the sorrow that comes with a heavy financial debt.
  fore-bemoanèd moan past grief.
13 **dear friend** the youth.
14 The dearness of the friend compensates for any heartache that the poet might feel.

31

1 **bosom** heart.
2 **lacking** not having. This refers to hearts and could mean lacking in heart, i.e. cowardly; alternatively, the poet believes his friends to be dead because he lacks their love.
3–4 The poet's love lies buried in the youth's heart, along with the friends he thought had died. Ironically, the youth then unites the poet with his friends.
5 **obsequious** dutiful.
6 **dear religious love** tender and reverent affection.
  stol'n tears that are paid.
7 **interest** the interest on the metaphorical debt that is due to the dead friends.
8 **removed** absent.
9 Love lives on in the bosom of the youth.

10 The implication is that the poet's past victories (*trophies*) in love have been transferred to the youth.
11 **parts of me** parts of my love.
12 **due of many** debt owed to many.
13 **images** perhaps suggesting that old loves were false compared to the love that the poet holds for the youth.
14 The youth possesses the love of everyone who has ever loved the poet: thereby possessing the innermost part of the poet himself.

32

1 **well-contented day** the day when the poet has fully repaid his debt.
2 **churl Death** death is personified as a lowly figure.
3 **by fortune** by good fortune.
  resurvey reread.
4 **rude lines** poor or unpolished lines of verse.
  lover friend (see Sonnet 31:10).
5 **bett'ring of the time** with time, all will be better.
6 **outstripped** bettered.
  every pen every other poet's verse.
7 **Reserve** preserve.
  for my love for those loved and those that have loved.
  rhyme the art of verse-making.
8 Bettered (*outstripped*) by those of greater fortune or, indeed, of greater artistic worth.
9 **vouchsafe me** grant me.
10 **growing age** an age when art – in particular, poetry – is developing in stature.
11 **dearer birth** more deserving offspring.
12 **march in ranks** a military image, suggesting keeping in step with (with a play on the notion of a metrical foot).
  better equipage the more worthy poetic advances.
13 **poets better prove** poets turn out to be better.
14 The poet will read the more worthy poets' work because of the value of their lines; he will read the youth's out of love.

33

1 **Full**   very.
2 Like a monarch, the sun flatters all it surveys.
3 **golden face**   reference to the face of the sun.
4 **heavenly alchemy**   celestial gold, the notion being that the sun is a true alchemist, and not the false 'magician' who claimed able to turn base metal into gold.
5 **Anon permit**   soon allow.
   basest   (1) lowliest, as opposed to the lofty status of the monarch sun, (2) darkest, in terms of morals and (3) of the metals, referring, once again, to alchemy.
   ride   move.
6 **rack**   clouds.
   celestial   heavenly.
7 **forlorn**   miserable and wretched.
   visage   face.
8 **disgrace**   disfigurement.
9 **my sun**   the youth, who is compared to the shining sun.
11 **alack**   alas.
12 **region**   the sun's region is in the upper sky.
13 **no whit**   not at all.
14 **Suns of the world**   (1) the better men of the world, on a par with the sun, or (2) lesser mortals, with a pun on 'suns' to mean 'sons'.
   staineth   the sun does not always shine gloriously; taken as a metaphor, the youth also stains the poet with his immoral treatment of him.

34

1–2 Shakespeare taps into the well-known Elizabethan proverb, 'Although the sun shines, leave not your cloak at home' (Tilley, S968).
3 **base clouds**   see Sonnet 33:5.
4 **brav'ry**   courage and splendour.
   rotten smoke   referring to the myth that clouds carried vapours that could be harmful, and even bring plague.

5 **thou break**   break through the cloud.
6 **rain**   tears.
7 **salve**   ointment.
8 Refers, again, to a contemporary proverb, 'Thou the wound be
   healed yet the scar remains' (Tilley, S929).
9 **shame**   remorse.
11 **sorrow**   refers to the shame of line 9.
12 **cross**   refers to the poet bearing the affliction, as Christ did in
   carrying the cross upon which he was to be crucified.
13 **pearl**   pearls were considered both a jewel and a soothing
   medicine when crushed.
14 **rich**   valuable.
   ransom all ill deeds   a religious metaphor: as Christ redeemed
   the sins of mankind, so do the youth's tears redeem him in the
   eyes of the poet.

35

1 **No more be grieved**   (1) no longer grieve and (2) have no
   greater grief.
2 **Roses have thorns**   relates to the proverb, 'No rose without a
   thorn' (Tilley, R182).
   silver fountains mud   beneath the silvery glimmer of moving
   water lies mud.
3 **stain**   darken, both literally and morally; as clouds were
   thought to carry disease (Sonnet 33:14), eclipses were thought
   to be portents of doom.
4 Proverbial: 'The canker soonest eats the fairest rose' (Tilley,
   C56); the bud in question is the youth.
5 **All men make faults**   proverbial: 'Every man has his faults'
   (Tilley, M116).
6 **Authorizing**   a legal image, meaning to sanction.
   with compare   the youth's misdemeanour (trespass) is
   compared with the sins of others.
7 By excusing (*salving*) the youth, the poet corrupts himself.
8 A commonly debated line, which appears to be ambiguous in
   its meaning: (1) excusing the youth's sins when they do not
   deserve it or (2) offering more excuses than the sins require.

9 To defend the youth will require the power of reason.
10 A paradox, in that the legal adversary is also the legal representative.
11 **lawful plea commence** to put forward a legal plea.
12 **civil war** war within oneself.
13 **accessary** a suggestion that the poet is partly to blame for allowing the youth to treat him ill.
14 **sourly robs from me** the youth has injured the poet most painfully.

36

1 **Let me confess** the poet wishes to declare his own guilt (with a legal undertone, perhaps).
  twain two separate human beings.
2 **our undivided loves** inseparable.
3 **those blots** those sins.
4 **borne** carry.
  alone without the youth.
5 **respect** motive.
6 **separable spite** an injury that separates them.
7 **love's sole effect** love transforms two people into one.
8 **steal sweet hours** being separated means that the two of them are no longer one and are unable to enjoy each other's company.
9 **not evermore** ever, in the future.
10 **bewailèd guilt** the shame that the poet has felt, presumably because he does not enjoy the same social standing as the youth.
11 **public kindness** kindness in the public arena.
12 unless the youth is willing to blemish his own reputation, by lowering his social status.
13 **in such sort** to such an extent.
14 The youth's good reputation is also the poet's good reputation.

37

  3 **made lame**   metaphorically speaking, the poet is physically inferior to the sprightly youth.
     Fortune's dearest spite   the coming of age (compare with Sonnet 36:6, *separable spite*).
  4 **of**   from.
     worth and truth   worthiness and constancy.
5–6   The youth's positive characteristics are listed.
  7 **Entitled in**   having a right to.
     thy parts   the youth's gifts.
  8 The poet makes his love for the youth stronger by grafting it onto the youth's worthiness (a horticultural metaphor, indicating that the poet's love grows out of the pride he feels in the youth's gifts (*parts*).
 10 **shadow**   It was considered that the shadow was the product of the more superior substance; however, this line offers the opposite meaning, in that the image that the poet has of the youth has given the former a most definite sense of worth.
 11 **sufficed**   satisfied.
 12 **glory**   honour.
 13 **Look what**   whatever.
 14 **then ten times happy me**   loving the youth – and even deceiving himself that his love is returned – brings the poet much contentment.

38

  1 **my Muse**   the creative power that inspires the poet to write.
     want subject to invent   lack a subject for in the youth himself.
  2 **While thou dost breathe**   while the youth lives and inspires.
  3 **Thine own sweet argument**   the youth himself.
  4 **vulgar paper**   crude poem.
     rehearse   repeat.
  5 **aught**   anything, or nothing.
  6 **stand against thy sight**   comes into view.

7 **dumb**   lacking in verbosity.
  to thee   about the youth.
8 **give invention light**   illuminate.
9 **the tenth Muse**   In classical mythology, there were nine female muses; perhaps the suggestion here is that the addressee is not female.
10 **rhymers**   poor poets, whose skill comes only in the rhyme.
   invocate   invoke.
11 **he that calls on thee**   the poet that invokes the youth as his Muse.
12 **Eternal numbers**   poems that will last for all eternity.
13 **slight**   unworthy.
   these curious days   days of critical poetry reading.
14 **pain**   effort.

39

1 The poet considers how he might best praise the youth, without praising himself at the same time.
2 **the better part of me**   Philip Sidney coined the proverbial phrase, 'my better half' (Tilley, H49).
3 By seeing the youth and he as one, the poet must, of necessity, praise himself in any praise of his love.
4 **mine own**   my own praise.
5 **Even for this**   because of this.
6 **single one**   unity.
8 **That due**   what is owed to the youth.
9 **O absence**   the addressee becomes the concept, absence, which is closely aligned with the youth.
10–11 The poet's leisure time would be less than sweet (*sour*) if he were not able (given *sweet leave*) to dream about (*entertain the time with thoughts of*) the youth.
13–14 The poet feels that his romantic verse brings the youth close to him, although he is absent.

40

Sonnets 40–42 concern themselves with how the youth has betrayed the poet by having a romantic relationship with the poet's mistress. The love-triangle is established.

1 **all my loves**   all those individuals that I love and all the love that I have given to them.
2 **then**   meaning both 'therefore' and 'at that point in time'.
3–4 The young man has already had the poet's full capacity of love, such that it is impossible to find more: a 'more' that is deemed less than 'true' (false) by implication.
5 **for my love thou my love receivest**   in return for my (the poet's) love, the youth has had sex with another of the poet's loves. The verb *receivest* sees the youth as a passive victim in the act.
6 Rather ironic, as the poet suggests that the youth enjoys the dark lady out of love for him.
7 **this self deceivest**   the youth may well deceive himself, but the poet does not.
8 **wilful**   stubborn and lustful. See Sonnets 135 and 136.
9–10 Again, the poet offers the youth absolution, despite the latter having stolen what little the poet has in life; *my poverty* could refer adversely to the dark lady.
11–12 It is more difficult to suffer a wrong committed by a loved one, than an enemy.
13 **Lascivious grace**   wanton charm; an oxymoron (apparent contradiction in terms), to complement *ill well*.
14 **spites**   malice.

41

This sonnet follows on from the last. It is a little more critical of the youth, but ultimately still excuses him by blaming his beauty and straying youth.

 1 **pretty** (1) young and attractive, and (2) wanton, and therefore
   a tempter.
 3 **befits** refers to the wrongs in line 1.
 4 The youth's beauty and young age incite temptation.
 5 In Sonnet 40:9, the reference to gentle suggests both high status
   and 'tenderness'. Here, it carries connotations of Shakespeare's
   plays *I Henry VI* 5:3:79 and *Titus Andronicus* 2:1:83–4.
 6 **to be assailèd** worthy of seduction.
 7 **woman's son** any man.
 8 **sourly** cruelly.
 9 **Ay me, but yet** this change in tone marks the break between
   the octave and sestet.
   thou mightst my seat forbear the poet insists that the youth
   had a choice and ought not to have taken his place in
   possessing the dark lady.
10–12 Beauty and straying youth are personified, suggesting that the
   youth believes that he has no free will: rather, he has been led
   to lust (*riot*) and forced to break a twofold truth.
13–14 The couplet, bizarrely, chooses to place the focus upon the
   youth's beauty, rather than upon his straying youth, as the
   cause of temptation. It is only this that leads the dark lady
   astray and prompts the young man to be false to the poet.

42

 1 **hast her** possesses her sexually.
 2 **loved** that the poet loved his mistress is now in the past tense.
   dearly fondly, tenderly; with a pun upon 'costly'.
 4 The poet states that he is more upset that his friend strayed,
   than that his mistress did.
   touches hurts.
   nearly deeply.
 6 The youth is excused, the notion being that he indulges in a
   love affair with the lady because it brings him closer to the
   poet.
 7 The dark lady indulges in the affair simply because she knows
   of the closeness between the youth and the poet.
 8 **Suff'ring** allowing.

for my sake with the poet in mind, since she knows that he loves the youth.

approve (1) to approve of her and (2) try her out sexually.

9 **my love's** my mistress's.

10 **found** recovered the love that has been lost.

11 In finding each other, the poet loses both his mistress and the youth.

12 **for my sake** (1) out of love for the poet and (2) excusing their illicit behaviour by professing a love for the poet.

13 **are one** the oneness of the youth and the poet is expressed here, and also in other sonnets.

14 **Sweet flatt'ry!** the sweet delusion that the poet suffers from.

43

1 **wink** close the eyes.

2 **unrespected** unappreciated.

4 It was believed that the eyes project light as well as receive it. As a result, the poet is guided towards the light, despite his eyes being closed.

5 The youth makes even the dark shadows appear bright.

6 In reality, the youth (the form behind the shadow) seems a most beautiful sight.

7 The youth's brightness is more vivid than the light of day.

8 **shade** shadow.

9 **blessèd** the sight of the youth both heals and enriches the poet's vision.

10 **living day** as opposed to the night, which is full of shadows.

11 **dead night** dead of night, meaning both in the middle of and at that time when the dead are most likely to walk the earth.

12 **heavy** a deep and unhappy sleep.
   stay remain.

13 All days are dark and sorrowful until the poet sees the youth.

14 **thee me** you to me (i.e. the youth to the poet).

44

1 **dull substance**   heavy and slow.
2 Malicious (*Injurious*) distance would not hinder the poet's progress (*stop my way*).
3 **space**   the distance between the poet and the youth.
4 **limits**   distances far away, the implication being that the poet would travel to the ends of the earth to reach his friend.
5 **my foot**   The foot represents the entire body.
6 **farthest earth removed from**   that part of the earth most distant from.
7 **jump**   leap over.
8 **think**   think of.
9 The poet bemoans that he is not thought, but merely dull flesh.
10 **large lengths of miles**   many miles.
11 Again, in the absence of the youth, the poet thinks of himself as flesh, and so made only of earth and water.
12 **attend time's leisure**   in terms of seeing the youth again, the poet must (1) wait for the time to come and (2) wait for Time (personified) to grant him that favour.
13 **naught**   nothing.
   elements so slow   earth and water (line 11).
14 The poet feels imprisoned by heavy tears: the heaviness coming from the earth and the tears from the water.

45

1 **The other two**   without the youth, the poet is merely earth and water, lacking the other two elements.
   slight   insubstantial.
   purging   purifying.
2 Air and fire are with the youth, wherever he is.
3 The first is air, while fire is the other.
4 **present-absent**   an oxymoron (apparent contradiction in terms), citing those elements absent from the poet, but present with the youth.
5 **quicker elements**   the speedier more vital elements of air and fire.

6 **tender** loving.
7 **made of four** relating to the common belief that the human body is composed of the four basic elements (or humours).
8 **oppressed with melancholy** weighted down with depression; melancholia was associated with an excess of black bile, a bodily fluid associated with earth.
9 **life's composition** the balance of the four elements.
recurèd cured.
10 **those swift messengers** air and fire.
11 **even but now** at this very moment.
12 **fair health** good health, with 'fair' perhaps also reminding us of the youth's beauty.
13 **joy** rejoice.
no longer glad the poet's happiness is fleeting, as he becomes despondent that the youth is faring so well in his absence.
14 **them** the messengers, air and fire.
sad once again, as heavy and melancholic as earth and water.

46

1 **mortal** fatal.
2 **divide the conquest** (1) share the spoils of war and (2) divide property, in the legal sense.
thy sight the sight of you (i.e. the youth).
3 The poet's eye wishes to prevent (*bar*, legally) his heart from seeing the youth's picture.
4 The poet's heart wishes to prevent (refuse *freedom of that right*, legally) his eye from sight of the same.
5 The poet knows that the true image of the youth lies in his heart, not in his eye.
6 The *closet* could literally refer to a small cabinet in which valuables were kept. It also relates to the area surrounding the heart, enclosing the youth's image so that not even the eyes can see it.
7 The eye (the *defendant*) rejects the heart's petition (*plea*).
8 **fair appearance** the youth's outer and inner beauty.
9 **To 'cide** to decide.

    title claim.
    impanellèd formed into a panel of jurors.
10 **quest** jury.
11 **determinèd** ascertained.
12 **clear eyes' moiety** that part that belongs to the eye.
    the dear heart's part that belonging to the seat of all emotion, the heart.
13 **mine eyes' due** what is owed to the eyes.
14 **my heart's right** what is owed to the heart.
    thy inward love of heart only the heart can appreciate love; the eye appreciates the youth's appearance only.

47

1 **league** an agreement.
    took made.
2 **now** compared with the competition between the eye and the heart in Sonnet 46.
3 **famished for a look** a metaphor, presenting the poet's eyes as desperately hungry to see the youth.
4 **in love with sighs** the sighs associated with the state of love itself, as well as those produced by melancholy.
5 **my love's picture** both the mental image and the real image of the youth.
6 **bids** invites.
7 **my heart's guest** the metaphor from line 3 continues.
8 **his thoughts** the heart's thoughts.
9 Either by means of the image or the poet's love of the youth.
10 **Thyself away** the youth, being far away.
11 The youth is forever present in the poet's thoughts.
12 The pronouns *them* and *thee* relate to the poet's thoughts.
13–14 If the poet's thoughts lie dormant (*sleep*), the heart will rouse (*Awakes*) the senses to better appreciate love.

48

1 **when I took my way**   set out on my journey.
2 **truest bars**   most trustworthy locks.
3 **unusèd**   left alone.
  stay   remain.
4 **From**   out of.
  wards of trust   honourable guards.
5 By comparison, the youth renders the poet's most valued possessions as trifling.
6 **Most worthy comfort**   the best source of comfort.
  greatest grief   paradoxically, the poet's most prized possession also gives him the most grief, since it is absent.
7 **best of dearest**   the youth is the best of the poet's most prized possessions, with an added meaning of the former proving rather emotionally costly.
8 **prey**   victim.
  vulgar   base.
9 **chest**   (1) a place to store valuables and (2) relating to the heart.
10 The poet knows that the youth is not literally present although he feels him to be.
11 **gentle closure of my breast**   the quiet confines of the poet's heart.
12 The youth may come and go as he pleases, both into the poet's life and heart.
13 **stol'n**   stolen; being absent, the youth may be stolen away from the poet, either as a victim or with consent.

49

1 **Against that time**   in readiness for that time.
2 **defects**   failings.
3 **Whenas**   at the time when.
4 **audit**   examination of accounts.
  advised respects   careful thoughts.
5 **strangely pass**   pass by like a stranger.

6 And barely give me a second glance.
7 **converted from the thing it was** changed from how it first appeared.
8 **gravity** the maturity and reason that comes with age.
9 **ensconce** shelter.
10 **mine own desert** either (1) my own merits or (2) lack of merits.
11 **this my hand** a reference to the sonnet, in the poet's own handwriting.
   uprear raise.
12 **guard** protect.
13 **strength of laws** the law is on the youth's side.
14 **why to love** the poet poses the question about the worthiness of any human individual to be loved.

50

Sonnets 50–2 focus on a literal or metaphorical journey, which takes the poet away from the youth.

1 **heavy do I journey** the poet's struggle is burdensome.
2 **my weary travel's end** the object of the poet's travel, with a possible pun on 'travail'.
3 **that ease and that repose** the lack of burden and rest.
4 The poet measures his woe in the spatial miles that separate him from his friend.
5 **tirèd with my woe** This metaphor suggests that the horse bears the poet's emotional burden, rather than his physical one.
6 **Plods dully** as a result of the burden.
7 **wretch** poor creature.
8 The speed of the horse takes the poet further from the youth.
9 **bloody spur** the spur draws blood.
10 **anger** although it is the poet's spurs that injure the horse, the personification of this mood means that he does not admit responsibility for his actions.
11 **heavily** sadly.
12 **sharp** painful.
13 **put this in my mind** it makes the poet think.

14 **onward** in the future.
    joy behind happiness lies in the past.

51

1 **Thus** in this manner.
    slow offence the slowness of his horse.
2 **my dull bearer** the poet's horse, which moves *dully* (Sonnet 50:6).
    speed Despite the horse's dullness, the poet feels as though he is speeding away from his love.
4 **posting** journeying quickly.
5 **then** at that point when it is time to return.
6 **swift extremity** the most extreme swiftness.
7 **spur** move ever more quickly.
9 **Then can no horse… keep pace** no horse can keep up.
10 **perfect'st** The poet uses the superlative form, in order to suggest a desire that is the most perfect.
11 **fiery race** desire races with the speed of fire.
12 The horse will be excused, out of love.
13 **wilful slow** deliberately slow, fitting in with the poet's current mood.
14 The poet proposes to run towards the youth, allowing the horse to move at its own pace.

52

1 **So am I as the rich** the poet sees himself as a wealthy man.
2 **sweet up-lockèd** locked up sweetness, i.e. the youth.
3 **ev'ry hour** regularly.
4 Examining treasure too frequently can spoil the pleasure of it.
5 **rare** special.
7 **thinly placèd** placed sparsely.
8 **captain** chief.
    carcanet a collar or necklace, set with jewels.
9 **So is the time that keeps you** in the same manner are you (the youth) kept separate from the poet.

11 **special instant**   specific moment.
12 **his imprisoned pride**   the splendour of the youth, which has lain hidden due to his absence.
13 **worthiness gives scope**   merit gives freedom.
14 Those who see the youth are triumphant, while the rest can only live in hope.

53

1 **substance**   essence.
2 **strange shadows**   foreign ghosts or beliefs.
3 Each shadow, or shade, has only one image.
4 According to the poet, the youth can project goodness and beauty.
5 **Adonis**   even 'rose-cheeked Adonis', the classical image of perfect beauty, cannot match that of the youth; see Shakespeare's *Venus and Adonis* (1593).
7 Similarly, should the youth's beauty be captured in a painting, it would far outweigh the physical splendour of Helen of Troy.
8 **Grecian tires**   Greek dress.
9 **foison**   abundance.
10 **The one**   spring.
   shadow   a paradox, as the argument is that the youth's shadow is not dark and ephemeral, but youthful and fair.
11 **bounty**   worth.
12 The youth can be perceived in every known beautiful and holy image.
13 **external grace**   grace of the physical, outer form.
14 The poet concludes that the youth can be compared to no one, since he has a *constant heart*, and this suggests that he is virtuous.

54

1 **seem**   suggests uncertainty.
2 **By**   because of.
3 **deem**   judge.

4 **For** because of.
5 **canker-blooms** blossoms of the unperfumed dog-rose, a metaphor for normal people.
  as deep a dye a strong colour.
6 **perfumèd tincture** the perfumed essence of the rose.
7 **such thorns** those thorns from other garden roses.
  wantonly playfully.
8 When the hidden buds of flowers are revealed in the summer breeze.
9 The flowers' beauty is only on the surface, since they lack perfume.
10 **unrespected** not treated with respect.
11 **Die to themselves** die alone.
12 **sweet deaths** roses were believed to die sweet deaths, as their petals could be distilled to make perfumes.
13 **of you** relating to the youth's beauty.
   lovely youth (1) lovable, (2) loving, and (3) lovely.
14 When beauty fades (*vade*), the youth's vigour will be preserved in poetry.

55

1–2 The poet claims that his poetry will outlive the valuables and palaces of royalty.
  3 **these contents** the contents of the poems about the youth.
  4 **unswept stone** ruined cities.
    sluttish time personified, Time is a *sluttish* housewife who has allowed her buildings to go to wrack and ruin.
  5 **wasteful war** a war that makes waste of towns and cities.
  6 Turmoil (*broils*) serves to destroy (*root out*) the mason's handiwork (*the work of masonry*).
  7 Neither the sword of Mars (god of war) or the fire of war will burn.
  8 **living record** this poem.
  9 **all oblivious enmity** enmity that is oblivious to the youth's worth.
 10 The youth will continue to advance (*pace forth*) and find prestige (*praise*) in the lines of poetic verse.

11 **eyes of all posterity**   eyes of all future generations.
12 **ending doom**   Day of Judgement.
13 When the youth rises on this day.
14 **this**   the poetic verse.
   dwell in lovers' eyes   lovers will use the youth as a perfect
   image of love.

56

1 **love**   the emotion.
2 **appetite**   lust.
3 **allayed**   satisfied.
4 **his**   its.
5 **So love be thou**   love is personified.
6 **wink**   close, the image being that they must no longer see the
   youth, since they are already full with his appearance.
7 **see again**   look, once more, with hungry eyes.
8 With regular viewing of the youth, the poet hopes that his eyes
   will never be sated (with to *kill* meaning to deaden the feeling of
   love, and *perpetual dullness* referring to blunting the keenness of
   this same emotion).
9 **sad int'rim**   interval of sadness.
   like the ocean be   a simile, where the poet compares the
   period of separation from the youth to the ocean.
10 **contracted new**   suggests that the poet and the youth are
   newly weds.
11 **banks**   it seems that the ocean is more like a river, with the
   poet and the youth standing on either bank.
12 **Return of love**   the sight of each other will hopefully renew
   their love.
13 **winter**   a conventionally miserable season, metaphorically.
14 The metaphor continues, with the youth's appearance being
   likened to summer, ever more valuable (*rare*) because it happens
   less often.

57

1 **tend** attend.
2 **your desire** the poet seems to suggest that the youth's love for him is changing over time.
3–4 The poet's time seems ill spent unless acting out the youth's wishes.
5 **chide** scold.
world-without-end hour endless time.
6 **my sovereign** using the imagery of Sonnet 33, where the youth was compared to the sun.
watch the clock wait with impatience.
7 The poet has to try to convince himself that the time apart from the youth is not painful; note the food imagery, as the absence is described as both bitterness and sour.
8 **your servant** the poet, who is slave to the youth's bidding.
9 **question with** ask questions about.
10 **or your affairs suppose** the poet dare not ask the youth about his conduct during their absence. Note that the word 'affair' did not carry sexual connotations until the early eighteenth century.
11 **sad slave** links to line 8 and the image of the poet as the youth's slave.
naught nothing.
12 **Save** except.
13 **So true a fool is love** with love once again personified, the poet characterizes him as more than a servant (line 8) or a slave (line 11); now, he is a *fool*.
will desire or male sexual organ. The quarto version capitalized this word, suggesting that it could refer also to William Shakespeare himself.
14 **Though you do anything** despite the sonnet expressing the contrary, it is in this phrase that we see the poet's real doubts about his absent friend's conduct.

58

1 **That god forbid** an appeal to the god of love.
2 The poet asks that he may cease thinking about the youth's behaviour.
3 **at your hand** from the youth himself.
   th' account an itemized list.
4 **vassal** slave.
   bound forced.
   to stay your leisure to wait until the youth returns.
5 **suffer** endure the pain.
   beck beckoning.
6 **imprisoned** imprisoning.
   absence of your liberty the youth's absence is a result of his freedom.
7 **patience-tame** an adjective, used to describe the controlling of impatience.
   bide each check suffer every painful blow.
8 **injury** hurting the poet directly.
9 **where you list** wherever you (the youth) wish.
10 **privilege** allot.
11 **To what you will** to your own wishes, with a pun upon sexual desire.
12 Should the youth partake of any crime, it is up to him to justify it.
13 The poet realizes that he is expected to wait for the youth; note the pun upon *wait* and *waiting*, once more alluding to him as the youth's slave.
14 Should the poet choose to wait for the youth, he cannot blame him for any misdemeanours performed in his absence.

59

1–2 The notion is that life is a succession of continuous, repetitive cycles (see Ecclesiastes 1:9).
2–4 The image is of the brain as a womb, giving birth to ideas.
  3 **amiss** in the wrong way.

4 The concept of a past child, being a burden to life once more.

5 **record** memory.

6 **five hundred courses of the sun** a long time ago.

7 **antique** ancient.

8 Since the time when thoughts could be expressed in writing.

9 **old world** ancient writers. This line is a paradox, suggesting that reading is a process of hearing through sight.

10 **composèd wonder of your frame** the youth's body would have provided substance enough.

11 **mended** amended, improved.

12 **revolution be the same** the time now is the same as it was then.

14 **worse** the implication is that the youth's beauty surpasses all, no matter the age.

60

1 **Like as** just as.

2 **our minutes** with a pun on 'hour' minutes.

3 **Each** each wave.

4 **sequent toil** endless effort.

5 **Nativity** newborn child.

6 **Crawls to maturity** moves to old age.

7 **Crookèd eclipses** bent, or malign, movements of the planets.

8 **confound** destroy. This line alludes to the biblical burial of the dead, 'The Lord giveth, and the Lord taketh away' (Job 1:21).

9 **transfix** pierce. Here, Time is personified as someone who stabs youth, disfiguring its beauty with age.

10 **delves the parallels** digs parallel lines (wrinkles).

11 **rarities of nature's truth** perfect specimens.

12 There is nothing that exists that could possibly escape the hand of Time, with the scythe being Time's metaphorical destructive weapon.

13 **to times in hope** until more hopeful times.

14 **his cruel hand** a reference to Time's scythe.

61

1 **Is it thy will**   do you wish that.
2 **weary night**   night that makes a person weary.
4 **shadows**   images.
5 **spirit**   ghost.
6 **far from home**   a reference to the poet and the youth being separated.
7 **shames**   shameful acts.
  idle hours   wasted time.
8 **scope and tenure**   aim and purpose.
10 **my love**   the feeling of love, or the youth himself.
12 **To play the watchman**   to act out the man who patrols the night.
13–14 The implication is that the youth is taking other lovers while the poet is waiting for him.

62

1 **self-love**   narcissism, in terms of both the physical and spiritual.
  possesseth   holds.
  all mine eye   my sight.
2 **all my every part**   every part of the poet.
3 **remedy**   cure.
4 **inward**   inwardly.
5 **gracious**   handsome.
6 **No shape so true**   no body so beautiful.
  of such account   so valuable.
7 **for myself**   in the poet's opinion.
8 The poet favourably compares his own excellence with that of others.
9 **glass**   mirror.
10 **Beated**   beaten.
  chapped   lined with wrinkles.
  tanned antiquity   ageing as a result of the sun.
11 **quite contrary I read**   The poet sees things in the opposite way.
12 Such a narcissistic individual would be sinful.

13 Since the poet sees himself and the youth as one, he has been praising the youth all along.

14 **Painting my age** decorating his (the poet's) own age with the youth's beauty.

63

Exactly halfway through the sonnets to the youth, the number 63 is significant. Known as the 'grand climacteric', 63 was thought to be an age at which great life changes occurred.

1 **Against** in preparation for the time when.

2 **injurious** committing deliberate injury.
   o'er-worn worn out.

3 **filled** as opposed to *drained*. The quarto version has *fild*, suggesting a smooth surface (and not *lines and wrinkles*, line 4).

5 **age's steepy night** a metaphor that creates the image of time as a steep hill.

6 **king** the youth's beauty reigns supreme.

7 However, all the youth's beauties are in the process of vanishing.

8 **Stealing away** the youth's beauties are both (1) creeping away with time and (2) stolen away by Time.

9 **fortify** make a fortification.

10 **age's cruel knife** as with Sonnet 60:9, Time is depicted as having a sharp instrument with which to ravage youth's beauty.

11 **That he** so that Time.

12 **though my lover's life** having already established that the youth's memory will never fade, Time will be able to end his life.

13 **black lines** lines of poetry (as opposed to the *lines and wrinkles* of line 4).

14 **still green** forever youthful, even after death.

64

1 **fell** ruthless.

2 **rich proud cost** perhaps alluding to the ornate monuments erected for the dead.

outwork buried age to counter-balance the line, the poet
speaks of the ugliness that time has wreaked upon the dead.

3 **sometime lofty towers** towers that were once tall and imposing.
down razèd demolished.

4 Even the so-called everlasting brass is subject to Time's hand;
perhaps this refers to the vulnerability of even poetry.

5 **hungry ocean** the ocean is personified as greedy.

6 **kingdom of the shore** land, which is described as the ocean's
competitor.

7 **main** ocean.

8 The ocean's gain is the land's loss, and vice versa.

9 **interchange of state** exchange; there may well be a deliberate
second sense to state, referring to the pending exchange of
monarchs (James I succeeding Elizabeth I).

10 **to decay** a decayed condition or even death.

11 **ruminate** consider; the word sounds much like 'ruinate',
suggesting that the poet is still imagining the youth's decay and
death.

12 **my love** the experience of love, or the youth.

14 **weep to have** weep while possessing.

65

1 **Since** since neither.
brass the first in a list of those seemingly invincible objects
that Time is able to decay; this noun comes first, as it reminds
the reader of Sonnet 64:4.

2 **o'ersways their power** (Time) is more powerful than they are.

3 **with** against.

4 **action** beauty must act against Time; there is also a link both
to a legal action and to the military action (line 6).

5 A metaphor, suggesting that beauty and youth are as ephemeral
as the sweet breezes of summer.

6 **wrackful** causing wrack or ruin.

7 **stout** strong.

8 **but time decays** time ruins them, anyway.

9 **fearful meditation** imaginings full of dread.

10 **best jewel** the youth is a beautiful jewel.

11 **his swift foot**   Time is personified as a runner, who can outrun anyone.

12 **spoil**   destroy.

13 **might**   force.

14 **in black ink my love**   poetry will keep the poet's emotions, as well as the beauty of the youth, alive.

66

1 **Tired with**   tired of.

2 **desert**   the deserving.

3 The poet refers to the rich, whose worthless selves are adorned in magnificent finery.

4 **unhappily forsworn**   either (1) those who have taken vows and broken them against their better judgement or (2) those vow-takers whose faith has been broken by others.

5 Honour that has been placed wrongly (*misplaced*) on undeserving individuals.

6 **maiden virtue rudely strumpeted**   the virtuous wrongly accused of, or involved in, whoredom.

7 **right perfection**   absolute perfection.

8 **limping sway**   authority undermined by weakness.

9 The censorship of art and literature.

10 **doctor-like**   acting as one who is learned in his field.

11 Truth wrongly called (*miscalled*) stupidity (*simplicity*).

12 In military terms, this metaphor has good under the authority of the wicked captain (*captain ill*).

13 **Tired with**   echoing the opening words, the image is of ongoing weariness.

14 **to die**   if I die.
   I leave my love alone   I leave my beloved on his own.

67

1 **with infection**   the youth is both infected by the hypocrisy of society and by his own morals.

2 **grace impiety**   adorn wickedness.

3 **That sin by him**   so that sin through him.
  advantage   benefit.
4 **lace itself with**   to interlace.
  society   presence.
5 Why should other young men be able to look like the youth through the use of cosmetics?
6 **steal dead seeming**   such men merely seem lifeless, compared with the youth's natural beauty.
7 **poor beauty**   inferior beauty.
8 **Roses of shadow**   imitation roses.
9 **bankrupt**   because the youth is so very beautiful, nature has nothing left to bestow upon others.
10 **Beggared of blood**   lacking the blood.
  blush   to show itself vibrantly red.
  lively veins   living veins.
11 **exchequer**   treasury.
12 **proud of many**   nature is conceited about the many false beauties in her store.
13 **stores**   she stores up.
14 **these last so bad**   these past corrupt days.

68

1 **map**   the face, metaphorically imaged as a map, is representative of the whole body.
2 **as flowers do now**   a reference to natural beauty.
3 **born**   worn.
4 **inhabit on**   live on.
5 **golden tresses of the dead**   the hair of the dead was often bought for hairpieces; *golden* refers both to the colour and monetary value of the hair.
6 **right of sepulchres**   belonging to the graves of the dead.
8 **beauty's dead fleece**   the hair (*fleece*) of dead beauty.
9 **holy antique hours**   the sinless prior ages.
10 **itself**   referring to his cheek (line 1).
11 Not making use of another's beauty to supplement your own.
12 **old**   used or former.

13 **store**   keep in store.
14 **of yore**   long ago.

69

1 **parts**   outward beauty.
 world's eye   every onlooker.
2 **Want**   lack
 the thought of hearts can mend   literally, that heartfelt thoughts can alter; this means that even the imagination could not make the youth's beauty more perfect.
3 **due**   right.
4 **even so as foes commend**   even the youth's foes praise him.
6 **thine own**   your due.
7 **other accents**   other, less complimentary, comments.
 confound   destroy.
8 **seeing farther**   searching with scrutiny.
9 **look into**   investigate.
10 **that**   refers to *the beauty of thy mind* (line 9).
 in guess   by guessing, estimating.
11 **churls**   grudging men.
12 **weeds**   the fair flower that the youth shows outwardly is coupled with a rancid (*rank*) interior. Note the antithesis of the rose and the weed imagery.
13 Continuing the idea of a mismatch between body and soul, thus subverting the theory of physiognomy, in which the outer body was thought to reflect the inner beings.
14 **soil**   foundation, with a pun on the notion of baseness.

70

1 **defect**   flaw.
2 Based upon the famous epithet, 'Envy shoots at the fairest mark' (Tilley, E175).
3 **The ornament of beauty is suspect**   suspicion adorns beauty.
4 **crow**   metaphor for suspicion.

5 **So thou be good**   as long as you are good.
  approve   prove.
6 **being wooed of time**   loved by Time, personified.
7 **canker vice**   vice, described as a canker-worm (caterpillar).
8 **thou present'st**   you show.
  prime   youth, as the prime of life.
9 **the ambush of young days**   those vices waiting to ambush the young: another military image.
10 Either not having succumbed to, or triumphant in his victory over, temptation.
11–12 But, to praise the youth for being morally pure is not enough to prevent envy, which will always be there (*envy, evermore enlarged*); consider the saying, 'Envy never dies' (Tilley, E172).
13 **suspect**   suspicion.
14 **owe**   own.

71

1–2 The poet asks that the youth's mourning for him, after death, should last no longer than the tolling of the funeral bell.
4 **vilest**   in the quarto version, Shakespeare used the variant form *vildest*. G. Blakemore Evans argues that the 'd' form seems to extend the force and weight of even the superlative' (2006, p. 167).
5 **line**   line of verse.
6 **so**   so much.
7 **would be forgot**   would rather be forgotten.
8 **make you woe**   make the youth full of sadness.
9 **verse**   sonnet.
10 **compounded am with clay**   mixed with the earth.
11 **rehearse**   repeat.
12 **decay**   die.
13 Lest the world should consider the cause of the youth's mourning.
14 And mock both the youth and the poet after the poet's death. Sonnets 135 and 136 suggest that the youth shares the poet's name, William; consequently, the mourner and the mourned will become one.

72

1 **task you to recite**   ask you (the youth) to explain.
2 **lived in me**   was in me.
3 **quite**   altogether.
4 **nothing worthy prove**   (1) find nothing of worth or (2) demonstrate that even nothing is worth something.
5 **virtuous lie**   an oxymoron (apparent contradiction in terms), that suggests that the youth would have to invent good qualities for the poet.
6 Such lies will present the poet as more worthy than he deserves.
7 An image referring to the convention of suspending epitaphs on the hearse of the dead.
8 **niggard**   miserly.
9 **in this**   in this respect.
10 **speak well of me untrue**   speaking well of the poet must come at a cost – the youth must lie.
11 **My name be**   let my name be.
13 **I bring forth**   in terms of the poet's writings or deeds.
14 The youth ought also to be ashamed, as he too loves worthless things.

73

1 **time of year**   autumn or winter, metaphorically the time of old age.
2 **yellow leaves**   another metaphor, suggesting that the time when leaves begin to change colour (in autumn) sees the onset of approaching old age.
3 **shake against**   move in response to.
4 **Bare ruined choirs**   both (1) the now bare tree branches, which had been the haunts of songbirds in the summertime and (2) the now desolate monasteries, left so by Henry VIII's dissolution of them.
5 **twilight of such day**   the light that is left at the end of every day.
7 **black night**   a metaphor for death.
8 **Death's second self**   a metaphor for sleep.

seals up all in rest   a reference to (1) being encased in death's coffin or (2) the closing of the eyes in sleep.

9 **glowing of such fire**   the remaining embers of the fire.

11 **it**   life or love.

12 Ironically, as time once brought beauty to fruition, so it must destroy.

13 The youth realizes this, so it persuades him to love with more vigour.

14 **leave**   let go of. Literally refers to the youth leaving the poet; there is also a pun on the word, referring once again to the 'leaves' of line 2.

74

1 The youth is encouraged to remain happy (*be contented*) despite the poet's death (*fell arrest*).

2 **Without all bail**   a metaphor, suggesting that death is impossible to stop (as it is impossible to be released from prison).

3 **some interest**   the poet's poetry gives his life some worth.

4 **memorial**   memory.
   still with thee shall stay   the poet's poetry will immortalize him in the youth's mind.

5 **reviewest**   see.
   review   see again.

6 **very part**   true part.

7 This line alludes to the burial service.

9 **the dregs of life**   after death, the spirit remains, while the body (*the dregs*) is lost.

11 **wretch**   death is personified.

12 **rememberèd**   (1) recollected and (2) a body put back together, in terms of its member parts.

13 A body's true value lies on the inside (i.e. the spirit).

14 **that is this**   the spirit (*that*) is the poet's poetry (*this*).

75

1 **as food to life**   a simile, which compares the youth to the poet's daily nourishment.
2 **sweet seasoned showers**   continuing the simile, as the youth's value is compared to the showers of spring.
3 For the *peace* that love will bring to the poet, he chooses to endure the *strife*; note the pairing of these two contrasting words.
4 As a miser both values and feels anxious about his treasure, so too does the poet value the youth's affections.
5 **proud as an enjoyer**   proud to possess (both wealth and love).
6 **Doubting**   afraid that.
7 **counting best**   reckoning it to be best.
8 Then, even better than best, would be that the whole world would witness the poet's happiness.
9 **Sometime**   at one time.
10 **clean**   entirely.
11 **delight**   desire.
12 **must be from you took**   must come from the youth.
13 **pine and surfeit**   a metaphor, seeing love as either starving or suffering from excessive amounts of food.
14 **all**   the youth.

76

1 **barren of**   lacking.
2 **variation**   variety.
   quick change   meaning a change in style and structure, for effect.
3 **with the time**   moving with the times.
4 The poet wonders why he does not write using the modern (*new-found*) methods and combination (*compounds*) words.
5 **Why write I still all one**   why does the poet continue to write in the same way.
6 **a noted weed**   a metaphor, comparing a specific garment of clothing with a conventional writing style.
7 **doth almost tell my name**   the poetic style is so recognizable that it is almost possible to recognize the poet himself.

8 **their birth**   the origin of his words.
10 **argument**   subject.
11 **all my best**   the best that the poet can do.
   dressing old words new   re-presenting or rearranging words.
13–14 A simile, comparing the cyclical nature of the poet's verse and the sun's cycle.

77

1 **glass**   mirror.
   beauties wear   referring to the youth's beauty fading with age, with a pun on *wear* (were).
2 **dial**   sundial.
3 **vacant leaves**   blank pages of a notebook, as well as the notion that the youth's mind is vacant until experience is written upon it.
4 **this book**   the youth will learn from his own writing (i.e. his own thoughts).
5 With time, the mirror will present the marks of age.
6 **mouthèd graves**   graves which are open to receive the youth.
7 **dial's shady stealth**   shadowy movement.
8 **Time's thievish progress**   personified, Time steals youth.
10 **waste blanks**   the poet's poems might as well be blank pages, unless the youth decides that he will apply his image to them.
11 The poet uses a metaphor to compare the youth's thoughts to children; they are born, cherished and delivered into the world.
12 **a new acquaintance**   by reading his thoughts upon the written page, the youth will view them differently.
13 **offices**   duties.
14 With constant writing, the youth will benefit (*profit*) and morally learn (*enrich thy book*).

78

Sonnets 78–86 display the poet's fears that his love and literary patronage have been taken by a rival poet.

1 So many times (*So oft*) has the poet asked the youth to be his poetic inspiration (*my Muse*).
2 **fair assistance** the youth's help, both as patron of the arts and as a model of beauty.
3 **alien** strange.
  got my use has invoked the youth for the same purpose.
4 Other writers use the youth as their muse.
5 The beauty of the youth's eyes has commanded the talentless (*dumb*) poet to produce worthy verse (*high to sing*).
7 Can refer to either the process of 'imping' new feathers onto a damaged hawk's wing or the use of feathers in the poet's quill pen.
8 **double majesty** the youth's beauty gives the already beautiful lines of poetry a further grace.
9 **compile** poems he has written.
10 **Whose influence is thine** the poet's inspiration comes from the youth.
11 **mend** improve.
12 The poetry is further adorned by the youth's grace; there may be a pun on the word 'grace' if the youth is titled.
13 **thou art all my art** again, the poet insists that the youth is his only Muse.
14 Despite the poet's lack of wisdom, he is elevated to a higher position of learning because of his love for the youth.

79

This sonnet and the next acknowledge the work of the rival poet, who is producing much superior love poetry with the youth as his subject.

1 When the poet was the only one to call upon the youth (to act as his Muse).
2 **had all thy gentle grace** enjoyed the youth's favour.
3 **But now** this contrasts with the *Whilst* of line 1.
  gracious numbers are decayed the poetry is suffering as a result of the youth's actions.

4 **give another place**   give room to another muse.
5 **thy lovely argument**   the youth is, in himself, a beautiful subject.
6 **travail**   mental hard work.
7 **of thee**   about you.
8 The other poet needs no thanks since he merely steals the youth's beauty.
11 **in thy cheek**   a synecdoche, the cheek signifies the youth's whole body.
   afford   is able to give.
13–14 The poet concludes that no poet requires thanks from the youth; rather, the youth has already paid, in that he provided the inspiration for the verse.

80

1 **faint**   grow weak.
2 **a better spirit doth use your name**   a superior poet invokes the youth as his Muse.
3 **spends all his might**   uses his poetic talent.
4 **To make me tongue-tied**   such competition renders the poet silent.
5 **wide as the ocean is**   a simile, comparing the youth's worth to the unfathomable width of the ocean.
6 Having acknowledged the rival poet's supremacy, the poet goes on to image a military metaphor: he is a small, fragile ship, while his adversary is an imposing galleon.
7 **saucy barque**   a small boat, which is impertinent, considering its insignificance.
8 **broad main**   wide ocean.
   wilfully   adds to saucy, with the poet's boat being stubborn and insolent.
9 **shallowest help**   the poet's small boat requires only the smallest help to keep him afloat.
10 **soundless**   noiseless; also unfathomable, immeasurable.
   deep doth ride   moves on the deep water.
11 **I am a worthless boat**   the poet speaks of himself as being unworthy of rescue or support.

12 **tall building**   a lofty and impressive galleon.
13 **cast away**   rejected.
14 **my love was my decay**   the youth (or the poet's love for him) would then be the result of the poet's ruin.

81

1–2 **Or... Or**   whether... or.
 1 **epitaph**   a verse in praise of the dead.
 2 **rotten**   decomposed.
 3 **your memory**   the memory of the youth (*you*).
 4 **in me each part**   in the poet's case, he will be totally forgotten.
 5 **from hence**   henceforward.
 6 **to all the world must die**   the poet will be forgotten by everyone after death.
 7 **a common grave**   either (1) an ordinary grave or (2) a grave shared by many people.
 8 **entombèd in men's eyes shall lie**   the youth will be both (1) an eternal image in the eyes of the world and (2) a false image of perfection. Note that the two meanings result from the pun on *lie*.
 9 **my gentle verse**   either (1) the poet's poetry will make the base youth seem more gentlemanly or (2) the base poetry will be lifted to a gentlemanly level by the poet's Muse.
10 **o'er-read**   read over.
11 **tongues-to-be**   tongues of those people who are not born yet.
12 **all the breathers of this world**   all those people who are living now.
13 **such virtue hath my pen**   the poet's pen has the power and moral capacity.
14 **breath**   both the breath of life and of rumour.

82

Sonnets 82–85 continue the poet's argument that elaborate praise of the youth is unnecessary. Rather, his own plain and simple style marks a quieter, inner devotion.

1 **grant** acknowledge.
2 **without attaint o'er-look** without dishonour, the youth may examine.
3 **dedicated words** those words used to dedicate their poems.
4 **Of their fair subject** about the youth.
5 **hue** outer appearance.
6 **a limit past my praise** an area beyond the poet's ability to praise it in a poem.
7 **enforced to seek anew** forced to look for again.
8 A new creation born of better days.
9 **do so, love** the poet grants the youth permission to turn to other admirers' poems.
10 **strainèd touches** artificial strokes.
11 **sympathized** represented.
12 **true, plain words** the repetition of truly and true reinforces oneness of the poet and the youth, and the truth of the poet's words.
13 **gross painting** very exaggerated depiction of the youth; relating also to heavily applied cosmetics.
14 The youth does not need such metaphorical or literal embellishments: such would be an abuse of the poet's artistry.

83

1 Continuing the premise of the last sonnet, the youth is deemed to be beautiful enough without further ornament.
2 **fair** beauty.
  set applied.
3 **or thought I found** the poet seems to question his own beliefs about the description of the youth.

4 The worthless offerings that constitute a poet's conventional praises.

5 **slept in your report** neglected to praise you publicly.

6 **That** the case being that.

7 **a modern quill** an ordinary writing style.

8 The break in the syntax in this line suggests a further question mark over the worth of the youth.

9 **impute** consider.

10 **Which** refers to the silence of line 9.

11 The poet's current state of silence renders him incapable of misrepresenting the youth.

12 **When** whereas.
   others would give life, and bring a tomb those poets who seek to give the youth immortality, present him with death.

13 **more life** a better chance for immortality.

14 **both your poets** rival poets, perhaps indicating the narrator and one other, or more than one rival.

84

1 This opening line continues the debate about which poet praises the youth best.

2 **you alone are you** the youth is unique.

3 **immurèd** the youth stores up the beautiful qualities within his own single frame.

4 **grew** a reminder of the nature imagery, which once again implies the youth is the rose when compared with any other.

5 **penury** poverty. The play on the word 'pen' suggests that the poet writes about the youth in plain terms.

6 **lends** gives.

7 **if he can tell** if he is able to describe.

8 **so dignifies his story** by so doing, he will improve his poetry.

9 All a poet has to do is write down what is outwardly written by nature's hand.

10 **clear** perfect.

11 **counterpart shall fame his wit** an exact copy would make his work well known.

13 **You** refers to the youth.
14 It is the youth's fondness for flattery that is his weakness; and this, ironically, deems him less eligible for praise.

85

1 **in manners holds her still** the Muse maintains her silence.
2 **comments of your praise** commentaries on those aspects of the youth that are worthy of praise.
3 **Reserve** store.
  golden precious. The *golden quill* suggests an elaborate writing style or one that enriches what it writes about.
4 **precious phrase** the most valuable syntax.
5 **other** others.
6 **unlettered clerk** illiterate parish clerk, whose roles were menial.
7 **hymn** a pun, referring to both a song of praise and every man.
  that able spirit affords that talented spirits offer.
8 **well-refinèd** a style that is sophisticated.
9 **'Tis so, 'tis true** reinforces the biblical Hebrew prayer word 'Amen', meaning 'so be it' or 'in truth'.
10 **most** utmost.
12 **holds his rank before** maintains the top position in the hierarchy of love.
13 **respect** love, value.
14 **speaking in effect** speaking only through deeds.

86

1 The opening line continues the metaphor of the rival poets' poetry being as grand as a mighty ship.
2 **Bound for the prize** the ship's prize will be the youth.
3 The poet's thoughts are ready to be spoken (*ripe*), but the rival poet intimidates him such that his words are buried within (*inhearse*).
4 Making their *womb* (*brain*, line 3), in which they were conceived, their grave (*tomb*).

5 **spirit**   intellect.
spirits   supernatural powers.
6 **Above a mortal pitch**   beyond the pitch of ordinary humans.
struck me dead   struck dumb.
7 **his compeers by night**   his spiritual comrades, communed
with at night.
8 **astonishèd**   amazed.
9 **that affable familiar ghost**   that friendly attendant spirit; note
that the adjective *familiar* is often associated with the devil,
thus attaching a rather sinister element to the rival poet.
10 **gulls him with intelligence**   tricks him with deceit.
11 Those spirits cannot boast to have rendered the poet silent.
12 **sick of**   sick because of.
13 **your countenance filled up**   the youth's face provides the rival
poet with the perfect subject matter to repair any cracks in his
poetry.
14 **lacked I matter**   the poet has been left with no subject matter
to write about.
that enfeebled mine   which served to weaken the poet's verse.

87

The poet leaves the subject of the 'rival poet', which perhaps
marks a new phase in the sonnet sequence.

1 **too dear for my possessing**   a paradox, meaning both (1) that
the youth is too expensive for the lowly poet and (2) that the
poet loves the youth so much that he can never possess him.
2 **estimate**   value.
3 **charter of thy worth**   worthiness, both in terms of material
wealth and moral worth.
gives thee releasing   allows the youth the freedom to release
himself from the poet.
4 **bonds in thee**   claims on the youth.
determinate   terminated.
5 **hold**   keep.
by thy granting   with the youth's permission.

6 **riches**   worth.
7 The poet argues that he lacks the necessary worth for the youth's love (*fair gift*).
8 **patent**   right of ownership.
 swerving   turning.
10 **else mistaking**   or the youth has misunderstood the poet.
11 **upon misprision growing**   growing on the basis of an error.
12 **on better judgement making**   on second thoughts.
13 **had thee**   possessed the youth.
 flatter   deceive.
14 The poet can dream of happiness, but this disappears upon waking.

88

1 **set me light**   value the poet lightly.
2 And view my good points with derision.
4 And show you to be virtuous, despite the derisive remarks.
5 **weakness**   moral or physical weakness.
6 **a story**   a narration.
7 **attainted**   tainted; or accused/found guilty, in the legal sense.
8 **That**   so that.
 losing me   destroying my (the poet's) reputation.
9 **a gainer**   one who gains.
10 **bending**   turning.
11 By repeating all the insults (*injuries*) that the youth has thrown at him.
12 The youth will be advantaged; as will be the poet, who believes himself to be at one with his love.
13 **so**   totally.
14 In order that the youth's reputation be preserved, the poet will soil his own.

89

1 **Say that**   argue that.
2 **comment**   enlarge upon.

3 Should the youth argue that the poet is lame, the latter will limp (*halt*).
4 **reasons** arguments.
5 **disgrace me half so ill** discredit me half as badly.
6 To find a cause for your desire to leave me.
7 **knowing thy will** knowing his own mind; or, perhaps, knowing the poet, there is a pun on 'Will'.
8 The poet will suppress (*strangle*) any signs of knowing the youth.
9 **thy walks** the places where the youth walks.
   in my tongue the poet pledges not to speak of the youth.
11 **too much profane** too blasphemous.
12 **haply** possibly.
13 **vow debate** vow to argue.

90

1 **Then** therefore.
2 **bent my deeds to cross** determined to go against everything that the poet does.
3 **bow** submit.
4 **drop in for an after-loss** attempt to deliver another blow after the poet has received so many.
5 **'scaped this sorrow** escaped from the pain of *the spite of Fortune* (line 3) or alternatively from the pain that the poet might receive at the youth's hands.
6 A military metaphor, suggesting the continued attack upon an already defeated adversary.
7 A meteorological metaphor, which suggests that worse could yet be to come.
8 Continuing the military image, the poet asks that the youth not draw out (*linger out*) any further pain.
9 **do not leave me last** do not be the last to leave me.
10 **petty griefs** other grief seems petty by comparison.
11 **taste** experience.
12 **might** power.
13 **strains of woe** levels or varieties of sorrow.
   seem woe appear to be terribly sorrowful.

91

1 **glory in**   boast of
2 **body's force**   physical power.
3 **ill**   badly.
5 **humour**   temperament.
  his   its.
  adjunct   associated.
7 **particulars**   relating to the pleasures listed lines 1–4.
8 **better**   improve on.
11 **Of more delight**   giving more delight.
12 **all men's pride**   all the items worthy of pride that men have in their possession.
13 **Wretched in this alone**   unhappy in only this.
14 **All this**   refers to lines 9–12.

92

1 **steal thyself away**   steal the youth from the poet.
2 The youth belongs to the poet for *term of life*, a legal phrase meaning for life's duration.
3 **stay**   remain.
4 **depends upon**   relies upon.
5 **worst of wrongs**   refers to the loss of the youth.
6 **in the least of them**   refers to the smallest indication that the youth's love is waning.
7 **a better state**   a happier state of being.
8 **humour**   mood.
9 **vex me with inconstant mind**   distress the poet with fickle mood swings.
10 **revolt**   applies to the youth's inconstancy.
11 **title**   entitlement.
12 **happy to die**   should the youth deny his love to the poet, the latter would be content to die; note that *to die* also alluded to the male orgasm, which was said to reduce the man's life by several minutes.

13 The poet asks what is so beautiful that it does not fear being
    blemished.
14 The youth may be false without the poet knowing it.

93

1 **So**   thus.
2 **Like a deceivèd husband**   Following on from Sonnet 92:14,
    this is a simile: like a husband who does not know about the
    infidelity.
3 Even though the youth's love seems true, if somewhat altered.
4 The outer appearance of love may appear to be true, while the
    inner reality may prove otherwise.
5 There cannot possibly be hatred in the youth's character.
6 By looking into the youth's eyes, the poet cannot ever know, for
    sure, what his love is feeling.
7–8 In many other men's hearts, their inner falsity can be seen only
    in mood changes and facial expressions.
9 **in thy creation did decree**   when the youth was created it was
    ordained.
11 **workings**   operations.
13 **Eve's apple**   a metaphor for the deceit of the youth; as the
    apple is beautiful on the outside but poisonous on the inside,
    so too may be the poet's love.
14 Here, the poet refers to the neo-Platonic notion of
    physiognomy, whereby outer appearance was thought to reflect
    the inner being.

94

1 **power to hurt**   beauty gives the youth the power to deceive.
2 **the thing they most do show**   the (probably sexual) activity
    that their attractive appearance suggests they could perform.
3 **as stone**   cold and unfeeling.
4 Unemotional, ice cold and slow to be tempted.
5 **rightly**   truly.

6 **husband**   keep, preserve.
  from expense   from waste.
7 They each control the face that they present to the world.
8 Others do not control their excellence and only administer it to the world (like a steward).
9 **summer's flower**   a vivid emblem of sweetness.
  to the summer   summer is personified.
10 It only lives and dies for itself.
11 **base infection**   disease.
12 **outbraves**   surpasses.
13 Refers to the proverb 'The corruption of the best is worst' (Tilley C668).
14 This could refer to the proverb, 'The lily is fair in show but foul in smell' (Tilley, L297). However, it may also refer to the expectation that a lily will smell beautiful because of its outward beauty; thus, an infested lily is worse than a weed.

95

1 **lovely**   beautiful.
2 **canker**   canker-worm (caterpillar).
3 **spot**   stain.
  budding name   growing reputation.
4 **sweets**   sweet things.
5 The many tongues that tell the youth's life story.
6 **lascivious comments**   comments upon the youth's sexual exploits.
  sport   pleasure.
7 **kind**   manner.
8 Despite the youth's bad behaviour, his good name exonerates (*blesses*) him.
9 **mansion**   house, abode.
10 **habitation**   dwelling.
11 Beauty serves to disguise the youth's potential for immoral behaviour (*blot*).
12 The youth's outer beauty means that he is only ever viewed in beauteous terms.

13–14 Metaphor, to suggest that the youth may lose his attraction
with further ill-use.

96

1 **wantonness**   lechery.
2 **gentle sport**   gentlemanly endeavour (presumably a
euphemism for wantonness).
3 **more and less**   of higher and lower social status.
4 The image has the lord's guests arriving as faults, but exiting as
graces.
6 **basest jewel**   least valuable gem.
well esteemed   well-considered.
7 **errors**   ill thoughts and deeds.
8 **truths translated**   transformed into good, moral thoughts and
deeds.
9–10 An image of the youth as a wolf in sheep's clothing; see
Matthew 7:15, 'Beware of false prophets, which come to you in
sheep's clothing, but inwardly they are ravening wolves'.
11 **gazers**   those who look on and see the youth's lamb-like
appearance.
lead away   mislead.
12 **strength of all thy state**   the power that comes from the
youth's beauty and rank.
13–14 The poet insists that, with too many immoral acts, will come a
poor reputation; and the poet's good name will be sullied along
with his lover's.

97

This is the first of two sonnets on the poet's separation from the
youth, with the seasons used as metaphors for the poet's emotions.

2 **pleasure**   that which lends the year pleasure.
fleeting year   the year that passes quickly.
4 **old December's bareness**   December is personified as an old man.

 5 **time removed**   when the poet was removed from the youth.
   summer's time   in the more plentiful season of summer.
 6 **The teeming autumn**   autumn is personified as a fertile
   woman.
   big with   pregnant with.
 7 **Bearing**   both carrying and giving birth to.
   wanton burden   the unrestrained, playful and probably dissolute
   offspring.
   prime   spring.
 8 Autumn is spring's widow, ready to give birth long after spring
   has died.
 9 **abundant issue**   all that nature offers.
10 Proves to be the same kind of redundant hope that orphans
   and the fatherless experience.
11 **summer and his pleasures**   personified as courtiers, summer
   and his pleasures are seen to wait upon the youth.
12 **thou away**   because you are away.
   the very birds are mute   pathetic fallacy; the birds are silent
   because the youth is absent.
13 **cheer**   mood, manner.

98

 2 **proud-pied**   beautifully variegated; April is personified as an
   elaborately dressed (trim) young man.
 3 **spirit of youth**   April is the month most associated with
   spring, when nature is regenerating.
 4 **heavy Saturn**   this deity was associated with old age and lethargy;
   of the four humours that were believed to shape an individual,
   'melancholy' was said to be governed by the planet Saturn.
 5 **lays**   songs.
 6 **in odour and in hue**   in smell and in colour.
 7 **summer's story**   a pleasant narrative, suitable for the telling in
   this bountiful season.
 8 **their proud lap**   the rich earth.
 9 **lily's white**   see the proverb, 'As white as a lily', (Tilley, L296).
10 **vermilion**   red.

11 **but sweet** only sweet.
   but figures of delight shapes of pleasure.
12 **after** like.
14 **shadow** image.

99

This sonnet varies from the normal form in that it consists of 15 lines.

1 **forward violet** the violet is forward because it flowers early and because it has stolen the youth's fragrance.
   chide scold.
2 **Sweet thief** sweet-smelling thief.
3 **love's breath** the notion that beauty comes from within; a fragrant breath suggested a morally pure person.
   purple pride a royal colour, to be worn with pride.
4 **for complexion** for colouring.
5 **too grossly dyed** the violet has too blatantly (by theft) taken the colour from the youth's veins.
6 The poet blames the lily for stealing the whiteness from the youth's hand.
7 **buds of marjoram** this aromatic plant is accused of stealing its colour from his beautiful hair.
8 **on thorns did stand** the roses, having stolen the youth's colours, must bear the pain for their crime.
10 **had stol'n of both** this third rose must be damasked (of mixed colour).
11 As well as stealing the youth's colour, the damasked rose has committed the additional (*annexed*) crime of taking his breath.
12 **in pride of all his growth** at the point when the rose had reached its most beauteous prime.
13 **vengeful canker** canker-worm (caterpillar).
   eat him up to death devoured the rose in order to kill it.
14 **noted** took note of.
15 **But** except.

100

1 **so long**   for such a long period of time.
2 **thy might**   strength.
3 The poet directly asks the Muse if she wastes (*Spend'st*) her inspiration (*fury*) on mediocre verse (*worthless song*).
4 This metaphor of dark and light, suggests that the Muse has ignored the worthy in favour of the base.
5 **redeem**   save.
6 **gentle numbers**   noble verse.
  idly   foolishly.
7 The ear clearly belongs to the youth, who will appreciate good poetry.
8 **argument**   content.
9 **resty**   stubborn.
10 **graven**   engraved.
11 **satire to**   be a satirist of.
12 **spoils**   plunder.
14 In order that the Muse might inspire the poet to counter Time's deadly weapons.

101

1 **what shall be thy amends**   the poet asks the Muse about the amends she can offer.
2 An allusion to truth being a vital part of beauty.
3 **on my love depends**   is dependent upon the youth, the poet's beloved.
4 **and therein dignified**   like the poet, the Muse is dignified (made more worthy) by the youth.
5 **haply**   perhaps.
7 True beauty requires no embellishment, in terms of further application with a pencil; this clearly refers to the youth's perfection.
8 The best (the youth) is termed so because it is pure and unadulterated.

9 The poet asks whether it is justifiable to be mute (*dumb*) because the perfect youth does not need praise.

10 Answering his own question, the poet insists that it is inexcusable to refrain from praise and he knows that the Muse must take responsibility for it (*for't lies in thee*).

11 **much outlive** live longer than.
a gilded tomb refers to the ornate monument built for a dead prince.

12 **ages yet to be** years to come.

13 **office** duty.

14 Poetry can offer only a seeming beauty, compared with the youth's present appearance.

102

1 **in seeming** in appearance.

2 **show** seeming.

3 **merchandized** a commodity.

4 **publish** publicize.

5 **but in the spring** early stages.

6 **lays** songs.

7 **Philomel** a nightingale. According to myth, Philomela was a princess raped by her brother, Tereus; she was then metamorphosed into a songbird (see Ovid's *Metamorphoses*, 6:424–74).

8 The nightingale was thought to cease singing at the end of July.

9 The summer is no less beautiful now (the metaphor suggesting that the poet does not love the youth any less).

10 **mournful hymns** sad songs, once again alluding to the tragedy of Philomela.
hush the night the notion that the melodious tunes of the nightingale make all other night-time noises cease.

11 The implication is that, when the nightingale stops singing, late summer produces the less than harmonious noise of wild birds.

12 Familiar pleasures no longer seem so enjoyable.

13 **sometime** sometimes or for some time.

14 **dull you** render the youth dull by constantly writing of him; consider the proverb, 'Familiarity breeds contempt' (Tilley, F47).

103

1 **Alack** alas.
what poverty what lack of substance.
my Muse brings forth create, delivers.
2 **That** in that.
having such a scope to show her pride having the beauty (in the youth) to best inspire her.
3 **argument** subject matter (the youth).
4 The poet's attempts to glorify the youth cannot make him more worthy than he already is.
5 **no more can write** can write no more to better the natural beauty of the youth.
6 **glass** mirror.
7 **overgoes** overcomes.
8 Making the poet's lines of verse dull and shaming him as a poet.
9 **striving to mend** attempting to improve.
10 Such attempts will only serve to ruin (*mar*) that which is already perfect (*well*).
11 **pass** end.
tend aim.
12 **graces and your gifts** the youth's attractive qualities and endowments.
13 **sit** be enthroned.
14 **shows you** reveals to you.

104

1 The implication may be that the youth is now showing signs of age, despite the poet's compliment.
2 **your eye I eyed** I saw you.

3 **seems** appears.
   Three winters cold three years have supposedly elapsed since the two men met.
4 **three summers' pride** the trees' foliage makes summer proud, or splendid.
5 **yellow** the colour associated with the season of autumn.
6 **process** progression.
7 The three hot Junes scorch the beautiful perfumes associated with the spring.
8 The youth was youthful (*fresh*) when the poet first met him and is full of vitality and young (*green*) now.
9 **like a dial hand** sundial.
10 **Steal from his figure** moves away from his outward show.
   no pace perceived with no seeming movement.
11 **hue** complexion.
   still doth stand stands still.
12 Refers to the unreliability of sight, as it judges only what it thinks it sees and not always the truth.
13 **age unbred** the ages yet to come.
14 The pinnacle of human beauty (the youth) is imaged as beauty's summer; the final point is that no future age will ever get to see such a beauty, since even the youth is not immortal.

105

Despite refuting the charge that he idolizes the youth, the poet goes on to describe him in threefold terms, which recall the Trinity.

1 **idolatry** worship of an idol; heresy.
2 **idol** subject of such devotion.
3–4 The poet claims that all of his sonnets are on the same subject.
5 **Kind** affectionate and good-natured.
6 **Still** forever.
7 **to constancy confined** restricted to the notion of fidelity.
8 **leaves out difference** this could simply mean that the poet's sonnets have no other theme but constancy (such that anything

'different' would be superfluous); should it refer to 'differences' between the two men, as in arguments or the fickleness of the youth, then this line could emphasize the poet's self-delusion.

9 **argument** subject-matter.

10 **Fair, kind, and true** each word expresses a characteristic attribute (an epithet), mentioned in some shape or form throughout this sonnet; the poet's reference to *varying to other words* may further emphasize the youth's lack of constancy.

11 **this change** this change in language to best describe the youth.

12 **wondrous scope affords** presents a wonderful scope for poetry writing.

13 Consider the proverb, 'Beauty and honesty seldom meet' (Tilley, B163).

14 **kept seat** lived.

106

1 **wasted time** ruined or unprofitable time.

2 **wights** individuals.

3 It is the beauty of the individuals that renders the poetry beautiful.

4 **lovely knights** beautiful knights, as opposed to the expected lovely damsels.

5 **blazon** in poetry, a commendation of physical qualities; originally a heraldic coat-of-arms.

6 For women, the hair and the breast would be found within this list; this, once again, exemplifies that the subject is a man.

7 **antique pen** the pen of ancient writers.

8 **master** possess.

10 **all you prefiguring** all those offerings foreshadow images of the youth.

11 **for** because.
   divining eyes only with speculation or inspiration; this relates to the idea that individuals have never before seen such beauty, needing help to appreciate it.

12 **skill** ability, or style (the latter being an obsolete form).

13 **these present days** now.

107

1 **prophetic soul** the fears generated by the mind.
2 **the wide world** a metonym (closely associated substitute) for the inhabitants of the world.
3 Can set boundaries for the regulation of my (the poet's) love for the youth.
4 The poet's love having been considered destined to come to an end (*doom*) after a finite period of time (*confined*).
5 The line tends to be read as a metaphor with Elizabeth I as the mortal moon having been eclipsed by death.
6 Soothsayers (*sad augurs*) have been forced to laugh at their own predictions, having once declared that the queen was immortal.
7 An allusion to the surety brought with the accession of James I.
8 **olives of endless age** the olive branch suggests a reign of peace and hope.
9 **balmy time** can refer to both the balm used to anoint a new monarch and the notion of healing.
10 **My love looks fresh** this new age also offers hope for the poet and his love; perhaps they, too, can begin anew.
 death to me subscribes the poet sees even the triumphant death bowing to him.
11 **spite of** despite.
 I'll live in this poor rhyme the poet can live on through his poetry.
12 **insults o'er** triumphs over.
13 **this** refers to the poet's poor rhyme (line 11).
14 **tyrants' crests** the heraldic symbol of noble families and monarchs.
 spent wasted away, destroyed by time.

108

1 **character** write.
2 **figured** displayed.
3 **now to register** the poet asks what is now to be recorded.
4 **dear merit** worth.

5 **but yet**   nevertheless.
   like prayers divine   a simile, linking the necessary praising of
   the youth with daily prayers before God.
6 It is essential that the poet enter into a recitation of the youth's
   excellence.
7 **Counting no old thing old**   allowing no word spoken, or idea
   written, to be hackneyed.
8 **hallowed thy fair name**   a play on the line from the Lord's
   Prayer, 'hallowed be thy name'; here, the youth is being held up
   for reverence.
9 **in love's fresh case**   by continually writing about the youth,
   the poet's love for him (and the youth himself) will appear to
   be young, new and vital.
10 **Weighs not**   gives no weight to, ignores.
   injury of age   the bodily disfigurements committed by time.
11 Neither does it heed the wrinkles that attack.
12 Makes *antiquity* (an ageing love, an ageing beloved, or the writings
   of the ancients) forever (*for aye*) his attendant (*page*); a secondary
   meaning could allude to the written page, re-emphasizing that the
   love and the lover will last eternally in poetry.
13 Finding the original idea (*first conceit*) of love, as it had been
   conceived (*bred*) in the youth's body or in the pages of
   antiquity (*there*).
14 The implication is that time may well alter the youth's outward
   form – signifying that their love, or the principle of love, is
   dead – but continued reiteration of what the poet has said so
   many times before will render the young man forever beautiful
   and their first love everlasting.

109

The first of two sonnets that focus upon the poet's willingness to
be apart from the youth. Despite what happens physically, he feels
that his soul will always live within the youth, as they are one.

1 **false of heart**   untrue to the youth.
2 Although the poet's own absence from the youth suggests that
   his passion (*flame*) has waned.

3 **easy** easily.
4 **soul** the seat of the human personality, wit, intellect, and emotions; that immaterial part.
  breast heart.
5 **home of love** the centre of my affections.
  ranged wandered.
7 On time and not affected by the intervening absence.
8 **water for my stain** a religious image, suggesting water to wash away any moral stains.
9 **reigned** prevailed.
10 **blood** ardour, passion.
11 **it** refers to *my nature* (line 9).
   preposterously absurdly.
   stained morally corrupt.
12 **nothing** valueless.
13 The poet values the wide universe to be worthless (*nothing*).
14 **Save thou** except you.
   my rose a form of address, suggesting the youth's beauty.

110

Sonnets 110 and 111 refer to the poet's public displays and the young friend's resentment of them. This perhaps reflects Shakespeare's own life as a playwright and actor.

1 This line follows on directly from the last sonnet, as the poet once again mentions his absence; the tone, however, seems to be less apologetic; the phrase *here and there* may well relate to the poet's sexual infidelity.
2 **motley to the view** a fool to the view of the world.
3 **Gored** wounded, dishonoured, or wearing 'gores' (wedges of multi-coloured fabric, worn by motley fools).
4 In new relationships, the poet admits to having come across old wrongs (probably infidelities).
5 **truth** true love.
6 **Askance** either obliquely or disdainfully; either way, being reluctant to look at truth head-on.

strangely   in an odd manner or as one unaccustomed to seeing truth.

7 **blenches**   sideway glances, with a secondary connation on the notion of straying from the path of righteousness.
another youth   renewed vigour.

8 **worse essays**   worse experiences of love.
proved thee my best of love   proved you (the youth) to be the best of all my (the poet's) loves.

9 **all is done**   the infidelity is complete.
have what shall have no end   the poet offers the youth his never-ending love.

10 **appetite**   sexual appetite.
grind   sharpen, whet.

11 **newer proof**   on newer friendships.
to try an older friend   to test an older friendship, by process of comparison.

12 **A god in love**   the youth is godlike in his ability to love.
confined   restricted.

13 **next my heaven the best**   the youth is next only to heaven in the poet's eyes.

14 **most most loving**   a hyperbole (exaggeration), perhaps designed to help absolve the poet's feelings of guilt.

111

1 **do you**   to be read as an imperative, 'you must'.

2 The goddess, Fortune, is blamed for the poet's misdeeds.

3 **That**   who.
my life   livelihood.

4 **public means**   public methods.
public manners breeds   which means that one is looked upon as vulgar, forced to wander *here and there* (Sonnet 110:1) in the public eye.

5 **my name receives a brand**   my (the poet's) name is stigmatized.

6 The poet's nature has almost been overpowered (*subdued*).

7 **like the dyer's hand**   a simile to liken the staining of a dyer's hand with the staining of the poet's public reputation.

8 **renewed** restored to the man he had been in the first instance.
9 **a willing patient** a simile that depicts the poet to be a martyr; he will suffer pain gladly.
10 **Potions of eisel** draughts of vinegar and honey, often used for plague victims.
11 **No bitterness** eisel was a very bitter drink, but the metaphor suggests that the poet will not think bitterly of the youth.
12 **Nor double penance** neither will the poet protest at a double penance, in order to exonerate his own guilt.
14 The sonnet ends with the poet's assurance that the youth's pity will be enough to remedy him.

112

1 **pity** compassion.
  th'impression fill heal over the scar.
2 **vulgar scandal** malicious rumour.
  stamped upon my brow the image of the poet as a convicted Roman criminal, with his crime stamped upon his forehead.
3 The poet does not care about his own reputation.
4 Provided that the youth will excuse the poet's misdemeanours and praise his good qualities and actions.
5 **all the world** everything.
6 The youth will tell the poet of the good and bad within him.
7 There is no one else who exists for the poet, nor indeed does he exist for anyone else.
8 As such, only the youth can change his sense of what is right and wrong.
9 **profound abysm** bottomless abyss.
  all care anxiety.
10 **others' voices** the voices of those other than the youth.
  adder's sense deaf senses; see the proverb, 'As deaf as an adder' (Tilley, A32).
12 The poet asks the youth to note how he so easily ignores the thoughts of others.
13 **in my purpose bred** in my thoughts.
14 Only the poet thinks the youth to be alive, i.e. compared to the poet, everyone else ignores the youth's reality.

113

1 **mine eye is in my mind** refers to the mind's eye.
2 And his physical eyes that guide him.
3 **Doth part** partly carries out.
4 **out** put out.
5 Physical eyesight cannot communicate any image to the heart.
6 **shape** body.
   latch perceive. Many editors read this word as 'lack', which gives an opposite meaning.
7 **his quick objects** rapidly changing images.
8 Neither can the mind's eye hold onto a physical image.
9 **rud'st or gentlest** coarsest or noblest.
10 **sweet-favour** beautiful.
12 **shapes them to your feature** (everything that the poet sees) transforms itself to the image of the youth.
13 **Incapable** unable.
   replete full.
14 The poet's mind is true, despite it making false what it sees.

114

1–3 **Or whether… Or whether** is it the case that… or that.
1 **being crowned with you** being made a king because of the youth's love.
2 Swallow quickly down the false praise, which monarchs are subjected to.
3 **saith true** speaks the truth.
4 **your love** your love for me, my love for you.
   alchemy the power to transform base metals into gold.
5 **make of** make out of.
   indigest ugly.
6 **cherubins** angels.
7 **perfect best** an example of tautology (saying the same thing twice with different words), which makes the phrase ever more exaggerated.

8 **to his beams** referring to the beams of light believed to emanate from the eyes.

10 **mind most kingly** the poet's mind is viewed as kingly, since it is crowned with images of the youth.

11 **what with his gust is 'greeing** what suits the appetite best.

12 This line refers to the servant's duty to taste the monarch's drinks to test for poison.

13–14 The final couplet has the poet insisting that he will always be the first to drink of his lover's beauty, whether the image is *poisoned* (untrue) or not.

115

2 **Even those** the very ones.

3 **Yet** however.

4 **most full** very intense.
flame a metaphor for desire.

5 **reckoning** counting.

6 **'twixt vows** between the promises of those that swear to something.
change decrees of kings time alters even the fixed laws that kings lay down.

7 **Tan** darken.
sacred worthy of devotion.
sharp'st intents keenest intentions.

8 **course** way.

9–10 **why… Might I not then say** why was I not then able to say.

11 **certain o'er incertainty** completely sure.

12 **Crowning the present** glorifying the present.
doubting of the rest apprehensive about the future.

13 **Love is a babe** Cupid, the love god, is depicted as a baby.

14 **To give full growth** to acknowledge as mature.
still doth grow grows constantly.

116

1 **Let me not**   I hope that I will never.
2 **impediments**   obstacles.
3 This line refers to the notion that true love is constant.
4 **bends**   turns.
  remover to remove   move in time with the moving.
5 **ever-fixèd mark**   like a beacon, or other navigation aid such as the stars, for shipping.
6 **looks on**   observes.
7 **star**   guiding star.
  wandering barque   lost ship.
8 **Whose worth's unknown**   the worth of which can never be reckoned.
  his height be taken   despite recognizing its altitude.
9–10 The poet's argument is that, despite Time's ability to destroy beauty (with its bending sickle), the love itself can never be destroyed.
11 **his**   Time's.
12 **bears it out**   endures.
  edge of doom   brink of either Doomsday or, more specifically, death.
13 **upon me proved**   proved against me.

117

1 **Accuse me thus**   the poet insists that the youth should subject him to a series of allegations.
  scanted all   neglected everything.
2 **your great deserts repay**   reward your positive qualities.
3 The poet admits that he did not call upon the youth's love.
4 **bonds**   personal ties.
5 **frequent**   familiar.
  unknown minds   strangers.
6 And the poet has given away the youth's right to spend time with him.
7 **hoisted sail**   a metaphor, which has the poet as a small boat.

9 **Book**   record.

10 **on just proof, surmise accumulate**   on top of what you can prove, pile up everything you suspect.

11 **within the level**   an archery term, meaning to take aim.

12 **wakened hate**   the youth's hate, which has been activated by the poet's misdeeds.

13–14 The poet insists that he committed all wrongs merely as a test of the youth's love.

118

1 **Like as**   just as.

2 **eager compounds**   bitter food and drink.
urge   stimulate.

3 **As**   also.

4 The notion is that we purge ourselves (*sicken*) in order to avoid future illness (*shun sickness*).

5 **ne'er-cloying**   never sickly-sweet.

6 **frame my feeding**   alter my consumption.

7 **welfare**   being well.
meetness   appropriateness.

8 **To be**   in being.

9–10 The poet admits that, by attempting to delay imagined evils, he created real ones.

11 **brought to medicine**   brought to the state of needing medicine.
a healthful state   what had been a completely healthy state.

12 **rank of**   sickened by.

13 **thence**   as a result.

14 **so fell sick of you**   the irony is that the poet's love for the youth is a disease, from which he will never find the cure.

119

1 **siren tears**   a metaphor, alluding to the mythological Sirens (part woman, part bird), who lured sailors to their deaths with their sweet singing.

2 **limbecks**   distilling vessels.
3 **Applying**   administering.
4 **win**   overcome his love-sickness.
5 **wretched errors**   sins, due to ignorance.
6 **so blessèd never**   never so blessed.
7 **spheres**   sockets; refers also to the star system.
   fitted   convulsed.
8 **distraction of this madding fever**   confusion as a result of maddening desire.
9 **find true**   discover to be true.
10 A superior subject is made even more so after the onslaught of evil.
11 A metaphor, comparing love to a ruined house rebuilt.
12 Corrected and, therefore, happy.
13 Another metaphor, implying the poet's spending on misdeeds has earned him a threefold investment.

120

1 **befriends me**   works to the poet's advantage.
2 **for that sorrow**   as a result of the former grief.
3 **my transgression**   the poet's misdeeds.
   bow   bend.
4 **nerves**   muscles.
5 **For**   because.
6 **hell of time**   time of hell-like agony.
7 **have no leisure taken**   not spared the time.
8 **weigh**   consider.
9 **rememb'red**   reminded.
10 **hard true sorrow hits**   true agony strikes violently.
11 **tend'red**   offered.
12 **humble salve**   healing ointment; perhaps referring to an apology.
13 **trespass**   crime.
   fee   payment.
14 The fact that the youth once injured the poet means that they can each forgive one another.

121

1–2 The poet plays with the proverb, 'There is small difference to the eye of the world in being nought and being thought so' (Tilley, D336); his point is that it is actually better to be vile, rather than falsely thought to be so (*vile esteemèd*).

3–4 **just pleasure lost** the poet concludes his argument by stating that the pleasures will not have been experienced if one is only thought to have committed sins.

5 **adulterate** wanton, defiled.

6 **Give salutation to** to salute, greet.
  my sportive blood the poet's passionate nature.

7 **frailties** moral frailties.
  frailer spies voyeurs who are more sinful than the poet.

8 **in their wills** in their opinion; with a pun on 'wills' to suggest sexual defilement on the voyeurs' part.

9–10 **I am that I am** the poet claims that he knows his own heart and that those casting aspersions upon it may well be casting their own immorality upon him.

9 **level** to guess.

10 **abuses** misdeeds.
  reckon up enumerate.

11 **bevel** crooked, biased.

12 **rank** rotten.

13 **maintain** continue to assert.

14 **in their badness reign** rule and flourish in their immorality.

122

1 **tables** notebook.

2 **Full charactered** fully inscribed.

3 **that idle rank** trifling writings and verses.

4 **all date** all time.

5 **brain and heart** the seats of both thoughts and emotions.

6 Have the power to function naturally.

7 **razed oblivion** an all-destroying oblivion.

8 **thy record** the memory of the youth.
  missed lost.
9 **That poor retention** referring to the notebook, which is a less valuable method of remembering the youth than the poet's brain and heart.
10 The implication here is that the poet's love for the youth is infinite and immeasurable.
11 As a result, the poet was brave enough to give away the notebook.
12 **those tables** the tables of memory.
13 **an adjunct to remember thee** an aide-memoire to recall the youth.
14 **import** imply.

123

1 **No! Time** The poet directly addresses Time, in an exclamatory fashion.
2 **pyramids** a term used to refer to any pyramid-like structure.
3 Are not new or extraordinary.
4 They are merely remodelled structures.
5 **Our dates** the length of our lives.
6 **foist upon us** push upon us.
7 **make them** claim them to be.
  born to our desire an object of our desire.
8 **Than think** than cause us to think.
9 **registers** records.
11 **what we see, doth lie** what we think that we see before us; a pun on 'lie' suggests an untruth.
12 Because time moves so fast, (1) history alters in the blink of an eye and (2) it becomes impossible to remember with any truth.
14 Despite Time's destructive nature, to man as well as monuments, the poet vows to be true to the youth.

124

1   **my dear love**   the poet's emotion of love.
  child of state   dependent on the state or the child of circumstance.
2   **for Fortune's bastard be unfathered**   disowned by its father.
3   **As**   because.
  subject to Time's love, or to Time's hate   at the mercy of
  Time, no matter Time's mood.
4   The metaphor has affection as weeds among Time's hate and as
  flowers when at the mercy of Time's love.
5   **builded far from accident**   built out of time's reach.
6   **suffers not in smiling pomp**   does not suffer pain.
7   **thrallèd discontent**   imprisoning sufferance.
8   Whereby the fashion of the time influences our behaviour.
9   **policy**   cunning.
  heretic   a dissident of the true faith.
10   Which works under short-term durations.
11   **hugely politic**   of great wisdom; note the change in meaning of
  policy (line 9).
12   **That**   so that.
  nor grows with heat, nor drowns with show'rs   neither grows
  (with Time's love) nor dies (with Time's hate).
13   **To this I witness call**   the poet calls witnesses to testify to his
  claims.
  fools of Time   lovers whose feelings are based upon cunning,
  (*policy*, line 9).
14   This line refers to those that die as martyrs, when they have
  lived a life of sin.

125

1   **Were't aught to me**   would it matter to me.
  I bore the canopy   the canopy is the cloth, carried on four
  poles, above the monarch's head as he walked; to assist in
  carrying it was considered a true honour. The opening line
  immediately conveys the notion that the poet would feel nothing
  if granted such a 'privilege'.

2 Honouring public displays of power with superficial outward displays (*extern*).

3 **bases** foundations.

4 Which do not last long given the onslaught of Time's decay and destruction.

5 **dwellers on form and favour** those who rely on the falsity of appearance.

6 **Lose all and more** lose everything they have and then find themselves in debt.

   paying too much rent paying a very high price.

7 A culinary metaphor rejecting plain foods in favour of more elaborate fare.

8 **Pitiful thrivers** an oxymoron (apparent contradiction in terms), relating to those who were once successful but have become wretched.

   in their gazing spent by looking on, destroyed all.

9 **obsequious in thy heart** dutiful in my love for you.

10 **oblation** sacrifice.

   poor but free a humble offering, but freely given.

11 **not mixed with seconds** without any inferior matter; a metaphor, suggesting that the poet is not giving his love to any other (who would be, by comparison, a lesser mortal).

   art artifice.

12 **render** surrender.

13 **suborned informer** a bribed informer or spy.

14 **impeached** accused.

126

This sonnet, with its twelve pentameters, rhymed in six couplets, marks the last addressed to the youth. Thomas Thorpe identified it as a non-sonnet, with a pair of brackets where the final rhyming couplet ought to have been. The ending is therefore inconclusive, a fitting poetic shortfall before the dark lady section complicates the narrative.

1 **my lovely boy** the poet addresses the youth directly.
2 **fickle glass** the hourglass held by Time.
   sickle hour that point in time when Time, personified, cuts down the ripe harvest with his sickle: in other words, the moment of death.
3 The suggestion is that as Time works on the youth in one sense destroying his body, the youth grows ever lovelier.
4 As the youth becomes more beautiful, it is the poet that withers.
5 The personification of Nature is able to overrule ruin (*wrack*).
6 As the youth moves forward in time, it is Nature who wishes to pull him back.
7 **keeps** controls, maintains.
8 **Time disgrace** dishonour Time (by overruling him).
   wretched minutes kill Nature destroys the power of Time, so substantial is her victory.
9 At the same time, the youth must fear Nature; he is in her debt and must serve her pleasures as though she is a monarch.
10 Nature may be able to hold onto her victory for now, but not forever.
11 **audit** final account.
   answered settled (the account).
12 A financial metaphor; Nature will no longer be responsible for the youth when she has settled (*render*) her account (*quietus*) to Time (by returning the youth to him).

127

The poet turns his attention to a woman – his mistress – whose complexion is as dark as her soul. This sonnet begins the 'dark lady' phase, which runs to the end of the sequence. The fair complexion of the Petrarchan woman (and, of course, the youth) is thought of as false if it is fashioned by cosmetics. The poet's mistress has a dark beauty, which he holds in high esteem.

1 **In the old age** in former years.
   black was not counted fair a paradox, which suggests that a

dark complexion was not considered to be beautiful.
2 If blackness was considered attractive, it was not called 'beautiful'.
3 **successive heir** inheriting the title of beauty.
4 **bastard shame** blackness is not the legitimate child of beauty.
5 **put on Nature's power** this alludes to women's ability to rival the hand of Nature, by applying cosmetics to make themselves more beautiful.
6 **Fairing the foul** making the ugly beautiful.
Art's false borrowed face the falsity that artistry can bring to the face.
7 **hath no name** has lost her legitimate claim on beauty.
holy bower shrine, in which to be worshipped like a god.
8 **profaned** cast out.
lives in disgrace disgraceful artifice, that presents itself as beauty.
9 **raven black** the suggestion is that the mistress has chosen her own eye colour to match her dark inter-self.
10 Her eyes appear to be like mourners.
11–12 Despite being an unconventional colour, the mistress's eyes mock those who are not beautiful and who apply cosmetics to make themselves superficially so.
13 **becoming of their woe** the eyes appear beautiful in their mournful state.
14 Everyone now says that true beauty has the mistress's colouring.

128

1 **thou, my music** you, who are my music.
2 **blessèd wood** wooden keys of the virginal.
motion sounds whose movement resounds.
3 **sweet fingers** of the mistress.
sway'st manipulates.
4 **wiry concord** the beautiful harmony that results from the plucking of wires.
confounds is delighted by.

5 **jacks** keys; that part of the instrument with which the lady's hand comes in to contact.

6 **inward of thy hand** the palm of the hand.

7 **harvest** the kisses.

8 **blushing stand** the poet's lips wait, blushing with envy.

9–10 The lips would willingly change from flesh to wood if only they too might be gently touched (*tickled*).

13 **saucy jacks so happy are** the impertinent keys are so blessed.

14 **Give them** let them have.

129

1 **Th' expense of spirit** the squander of both (1) the most vital energy and (2) semen.
waste of shame the shameful waste that such an expense entails.

2 **lust in action** lustful act of sexual intercourse.
till action until the act is undertaken.

3 **perjured, murd'rous, bloody** lust will lie, kill and be brutal to achieve its ends.
full of blame lust is the one to blame.

4 **extreme** excessive.

5 **Enjoyed** in terms of the sexual act.

6 **had** sexually consummated.

7 **a swallowed bait** when a fish or other creature has swallowed bait it thrashes about as if mad; this continues the hunting metaphor, but turns the hunter into the hunted.

8–9 The desire makes the pursuer frenzied (*mad*), an overwhelming emotion which continues even after consummation (*possession*) has taken place.

10 The lover is mad having had sexual intercourse, in the midst of having sexual intercourse, and in pursuance of the sex act.

11 **A bliss in proof** an extreme pleasure in action.
proved a very woe once experienced, leaving the man in a sorrowful state.

12 In anticipation, the prospect of sex is joyful; once the experience is in the past, it proves to be a nightmare.

13 **the world**   everyone.
14 **heaven**   of sexual ecstasy.
   hell   of guilt and pain.

130

This is classed as an anti-Petrarchan sonnet, as it reverses the conventions for praising a woman. Francesco Petrarca's Laura was flaxen haired, blue eyed, pale skinned, rosy cheeked, globe breasted, with red lips like Cupid's bows. This sonnet presents the mistress as beautiful, despite lacking the conventional image.

1 **nothing like the sun**   the mistress does not have eyes that can be compared to the sun, which suggests that they do not shine as would the conventionally beautiful blue eyes. We know, already, that she has dark eyes.
2 **lips' red**   the red of her lips.
3 The poet's mistress has breasts that are dark by comparison with snow.
4 The conventional beauty has hair compared to golden spun thread (*wires*), whereas the poet's mistress has black hair.
5–6 The variegated colours of the damask rose do not appear in the mistress's cheeks.
8 **reeks**   exhales
9–10 The mistress's voice cannot be compared to music.
11 **grant**   admit.
   a goddess go   deities were believed to be recognizable by the way they walked.
12 **treads on the ground**   unlike a goddess, the mistress walks on the earth like any human does.
13 **rare**   splendid, beautiful.
14 **belied**   described erroneously.
   false compare   deceitful, superficial comparison.

131

1   **tyrannous** pitiless (because of her beauty).
   so as thou art just as you are.
2   Cruelty comes with the good looks that engender arrogance.
3   **dear doting heart** the poet's own heart, which is dictated to by the mistress.
4   **jewel** a metaphor, which images the mistress as a most precious gem.
5   **in good faith** in all honesty.
6   **make love groan** make lovers groan with desire.
7   **To say they err** to say that they are wrong.
8   Even though the poet privately argues that the others are wrong.
10 **thinking on** thinking about.
11 **One on another's neck** in quick succession.
13 The poet decides that the mistress is beautiful (*fair*) in her looks, but immoral (*black*) in her actions (*deeds*).
14 The poet assumes that this is why such slander (as in line 6) ensues (*proceeds*).

132

1   **as** as if.
2   **torment me with disdain** tortures me with contempt.
3   See Sonnet 127:9–10.
4   **pretty ruth** agreeable pity.
5   **morning** a pun on 'mourning', perhaps suggests that even this sun is less than bright.
6   **grey cheeks of the east** the grey light of the pallid sun, rising in the east.
7   **that full star** Hesperus, the evening star.
8   **sober** sombre.
10 **beseem** become.
11 **doth thee grace** makes the mistress more beautiful.
12 **suit... like** make alike.

14 **And all they foul**   and all those are foul, ugly.
   complexion   skin colouring and disposition.

133

1 **Beshrew**   a mild oath, such as 'fie upon', 'shame upon'.
2 **deep wound**   terrible injury; referring to the extended
   metaphor (conceit) that suggested a woman's eyes were like
   darts, ready to pierce a man's heart.
4 **slave to slavery**   completely enslaved.
5 **from myself**   from my own true self.
6 **my next self**   the youth.
   harder hast engrossèd   more cruelly and completely
   monopolized (such that there is nothing left for the poet).
7 **forsaken**   abandoned.
8 **thrice threefold**   to be taken literally as 'multiplied by nine'.
   crossèd   thwarted.
9 **Prison**   imprison.
   steel bosom's ward   a jail cell for encasing hearts.
10 **bail**   redeem.
11 Although the mistress may confine the poet's heart, he asks
   only that he may be the guard of his friend's heart.
12 **use rigour**   torment; in other words, the mistress could no
   longer torment the youth, because the poet would protect him.
13 **pent**   imprisoned.
13–14 Couplet argues that the mistress will still torment both men – if
   the poet is tormented, so will the youth be, since he is in the
   poet's heart.

134

Sonnets 134–136 have become known as the 'will' sonnets, with
puns on this word being prevalent throughout.

1 **confessed**   acknowledged.
2 **mortgaged**   a legal metaphor; the poet is bound to the mistress.
   will   desire.

3 **so** in order that.

that other mine the youth (the other part of the poet's self).

4 **still** always.

5 **wilt not** will not allow the youth to be free.

6 **covetous** possessive.

kind both kind-hearted and loving.

7–8 Legal imagery; the notion is that the youth wooed the mistress on the poet's behalf (*surety-like*), only to become besotted with her himself.

9 The mistress will take everything that her beauty demands.

10 **usurer** the mistress is like a money-lender.

put'st forth all to use offers money only for profit.

11 **sue** both to (1) pursue for repayment of a debt and (2) woo.

came who became.

12 **my unkind abuse** either as a result of (1) the mistress's harsh treatment of the poet or (2) the poet's injury to the youth in allowing him to become involved in the situation.

14 **He pays the whole** the youth must now pay the entire debt, in terms of sexually satisfying the mistress; note the pun of *whole*, to mean 'hole' (vagina).

yet I am not free the poet is not free of the mistress's claim upon him.

135

1 **Will** desire. While other women may wish to have their desires fulfilled, the mistress has her Will (wishes and sexual desires; also perhaps the poet, William).

2 The references to the 'Will' being in addition (*to boot*) and excessive (*in overplus*) could well refer to the size of the poet's penis; also to the fact that more than one William may be involved.

3 **More than enough** again, with reference to his genitalia, the poet may be bragging that he has more than enough to satisfy the lady.

vex torment.

4 **thy sweet will** a reference to the mistress's vagina.

5 **whose will is large and spacious** an insult to the mistress, suggesting both (1) that her generous nature has occasioned her to have sex with many men and (2) that the *large and spacious* size of her vagina signifies how many men she has had sex with.

6 **once** just this once.

7 **will** intention.
  gracious graceful.

8 **my will** my desire.
  no fair acceptance shine the mistress will not accept the poet as a lover.

9 A metaphor, to suggest that the mistress should be able to accept another lover. See the proverb, 'The sea refuses no river' (Tilley, S181).

10 **store** stock.

11 **being rich in Will, add to thy Will** the poet addresses the mistress: being already full of desire should not dissuade her from adding to her stock.

12 The poet's desire, or penis, can serve to enlarge the lady's already large desire, or vagina.

13 The poet urges the mistress to stop saying '*no*' to fair beseechers, namely himself.

14 Consider all beseechers to be just one: the poet. Then the mistress will accept *Will* to be the poet's desire, his penis and his name (William).

136

1 **soul** the seat of intelligence and emotions.
  check chastise.
  I come so near both in terms of urging the mistress for an answer and coming close to her with sexual intentions.

2 **thy blind soul** either a soul that is ignorant or one that is blinded by passion.
  I was thy Will what the mistress was passionate for, in terms of being her William.

3 And the poet's passion, and penis (*will*), were allowed entry to the mistress's soul, and vagina (*there*).

4 **sweet** this could refer to either the mistress, who is sweet to the poet, or to the sweetness of the love-suit itself.

5 **Will will fulfil** literally, 'William, or sexual desire, shall be satisfied'.

treasure treasury, meaning vagina.

6 **fill it full with wills** the sexual implication is that the mistress should fill her vagina with penises.

my will one the poet places the emphasis upon his own penis (*will*) being the one that the mistress should choose.

7 **In things of great receipt** meaning the largeness of both the penis and the vagina.

with ease we prove we can easily demonstrate.

8 Alluding to *one* not being a number; essentially, it is 'none'. See Sonnet 8:14.

9 **number** total (of wills).

untold unaccounted for.

10 **thy store's account** inventory.

I one must be the poet has been the mistress's lover (if unaccounted for).

11 **For nothing hold me** you may esteem me to be nothing. There is also a pun on *nothing* (no-thing), meaning the mistress's vagina, which the poet hopes will clasp him.

12 **That nothing, me** that which is nothing is me.

a something sweet to thee an object that the mistress holds dear. Continuing the pun, *something* (some-thing) could well refer to the penis.

13 **Make but** make only.

14 The final line argues that, if the mistress's passion is her 'will', then she must love Will: as they are the same.

137

1 **blind fool love** the poet directly addresses Cupid, who is depicted as being blind.

2 **see not what they see** do not see the truth.

3 **where it lies** where true beauty lives.

4 The poet realizes that he has been interpreting what is ugly (*the worst*) to be beautiful (*the best*).

5 **corrupt by over-partial looks** the eyes are made immoral by their impartial view.

6 A shipping metaphor, imaging men being transfixed (*anchored*) in the inlet (*bay*) where all men ride at anchor; this image is clearly sexual, with 'bay' suggesting vagina and 'ride' the sex act itself.

7 **eyes' falsehood** the lies that his eyes are communicating to him.
hooks the small anchors that grapple the poet's heart.

8 **judgement of my heart** love.

9 **that** the mistress and her vagina.
a several plot a piece of private land.

10 **the wide world's common place** the place where all men go.

11 The poet questions why his eyes cannot see that the mistress is sexually promiscuous.

12 **fair truth** beauty and moral virtue.
foul ugly and immoral.

13 **In things right true** with regards to those who are truly beautiful and virtuous.
my heart and eyes have erred the poet's emotions and sight have failed him.

14 **false plague** the mistress is considered to be a disease to the poet, as she alters his interpretations.
transferred a shift (in desire), suggesting that the poet perhaps once loved a true woman.

138

1 **made of truth** morally true; there may be a pun on 'maid'.

2 **lies** both tells untruths and 'lies' with many men.

3 **That** in order that.
untutored youth unsophisticated young man.

4 **Unlearnèd** inexperienced.
false subtleties deceiving tricks.

5 **vainly** falsely, because the poet flatters himself.

6 **past the best** past the prime of life.

7 **Simply** foolishly.

8 **On both sides** for both the mistress and the poet.

9 **unjust** untrue.

10 The poet asks himself why he does not admit that he is no longer young.

11 **best habit** best attire; a metaphor for deception.
seeming trust appearing to trust.

12 Older people who fall in love (*age in love*) do not enjoy being reminded of their age.

13 **lie with** both in terms of telling each other flattering untruths and lying together sexually.

14 **in our faults** through our sins.
flattered be are gratified.

139

1 **call not me** do not ask me.
to justify the wrong rather ironic, as the poet has sought to do just this in Sonnets 137 and 138.

2 **heart** the seat of emotion and understanding.

3 **Wound me not with thine eye** the poet demands that the mistress not turn her wandering eye to other men while in his company.
but with thy tongue he wishes that she tell him about her other lovers.

4 The mistress should use her power over him directly and openly, without deploying any cunning policy.

5 **Tell me thou lov'st elsewhere** both (1) tell me that you love another man and (2) tell me that you love another man in a private place.

6 **Dear heart** the poet directly addresses the mistress.
glance thine eye aside look at other possible sexual partners.

7 **cunning** false stratagems.
might power.

8 **my o'er pressed defence** over-burdened resistance.
bide endure.

9 **Let me excuse thee** a paradox, as the poet now attempts to justify the mistress's actions.
my love the mistress.

10–12   Once again referring to a woman's eyes as darts that injure their male prey.

    13 **but since I am near slain**   because the poet is close to death as a result of his mistress's beauty and infidelity.

    14 **outright**   immediately.
        rid my pain   relieve the emotional and physical suffering.

140

    1 **press**   pressurize or oppress.
    2 **My tongue-tied patience**   my patient silence.
      disdain   contempt.
    3 **Lest**   for fear that.
    4 **pity-wanting pain**   pain as a result of the mistress being pitiless.
    5 **wit**   wisdom and discretion.
    6 Should the mistress not love the poet, she should take pleasure from telling him that she does.
    7 **testy**   irritable.
    8 Doctors give irritable dying men kind reports.
    9 To be given desperate news from his mistress would send the poet mad.
    10 Such a frenzied state of mind might well induce him to insult her (*speak ill of thee*).
    11 **this ill-wresting world**   this world which twists ('wrests') the truth.
    12 **mad ears**   the ears represent the whole of those hearing the slander (a synecdoche), but failing to interpret it as such.
    13 **belied**   the subject of slander.
    14 **Bear thine eyes straight**   the mistress is asked to look only upon the poet when in public.
        though thy proud heart go wide   even though her wandering heart ranges widely.

141

1 **In faith**   truly.
2 **errors**   defects both of beauty and morality.
3 **they**   eyes.
4 **in despite of view**   in spite of what the eyes see.
   is pleased to dote   is only too happy to become obsessed.
5 **tongue's tune**   sound of the mistress's voice.
6 The poet's own sense of touch (*tender feeling*) does not enjoy
   his mistress's crude and immoral caresses (*base touches*).
8 **sensual feast**   alluding to a banquet for the five senses.
   with thee alone   with only the mistress.
9 **five wits**   the five intellectual powers were said to be: common
   wit, imagination, fantasy, estimation, and memory.
10 **serving**   in the sexual sense.
11 **unswayed**   ungoverned.
   the likeness of a man   the shell of a man.
12 All men are just as likely to become the mistress's follower
   (*slave*) and pitiable dependant (*vassal wretch*).
13 **my plague**   both the love-sickness and his mistress.
14 **awards me pain**   inflicts pain upon him as reward.

142

1 **Love is my sin**   the poet's only sin is in loving his mistress.
   thy dear virtue   the mistress's virtue is promiscuity.
2 Both (1) the mistress hates the poet's sinful loving and (2) her
   own brand of loving is sinful.
3 The poet asks that his mistress measure her own love against
   his own.
4 **it**   the poet's love.
   merits not reproving   does not deserve criticism.
6 **profaned**   defiled.
   scarlet ornaments   redness; with an allusion to the red wax
   seals on legal documents such as bonds (line 7).
7 **sealed false bonds of love**   given kisses, which prove to be
   false.

8 Here, the poet accuses the mistress, not only of promiscuity, but also of adultery: she has stolen other women's husbands and the possible sexual satisfaction and children that were their due (*revenues of their rents*).

9 The poet asks if he may love his mistress in the same way as she loves other men.

10 **Whom thine eyes woo**   whom the mistress woos with her wandering gaze.

11 **Root**   plant.

12 So that the mistress's need for pity may be recognized.

13 **what thou dost hide**   pity.

14 By her own example, the mistress may well be refused pity.

143

1 **careful housewife**   conscientious housewife (pronounced 'hussif').

2 **feathered creatures**   fowl.

3 **swift dispatch**   haste (with *swift* acting as an intensifier).

4 **the thing she would have stay**   the fowl she wants to retain.

5 **holds her in chase**   pursues the mother.

6 **to catch her**   to catch her attention.
bent   intent upon.

7 **flies before her face**   as she is watching it, the fowl flies away.

8 **Not prizing**   not caring about.

10 The sestet opens by confirming that the octave was a simile, comparing the mother to the mistress and the child to the poet.
afar behind   from a distance.

11 **thy hope**   that which you hope for; the pursued.

12 **be kind**   both in terms of affection and in a sexual sense.

13 **thy Will**   the mistress's hope or desire, who is William.

14 **still**   silence with kisses.

144

1 **Two loves**   two beloveds.
comfort and despair   relating to the medieval concept of a good angel on one shoulder and a bad angel on the other, each vying

for the individual's soul.

2 **spirits** incorporeal beings.
  suggest prompt.
3 **better angel** the youth, who is right fair in complexion and morals.
4 **worser spirit** the mistress, whose dark skin and lax morality has earned her the description *coloured ill*.
5 The female evil works to pull the poet's soul to hell.
6 The poet is thrown into despair because the mistress is working to tempt the youth.
7 **saint** his beloved youth.
8 **purity** innocence.
  foul pride ugly desire.
9 **fiend** a devil.
10 The poet may suspect this, but cannot voice his suspicions.
11 Being absent from the poet, the youth and the mistress are friendly with each other.
12 **I guess** I believe.
  one angel in another's hell the youth is now in the evil world of the mistress; hell probably refers to female genitalia, whereby the mistress's vagina has entrapped him physically.
13 **ne'er know** never know for certain.
14 **fire my good one out** a metaphor for both (1) the mistress's eventual rejection of the youth and (2) his being given a burning venereal disease.

145

This sonnet is octosyllabic – the lines have eight syllables each instead of the usual ten. It is often dated earlier than the others, mainly because of what might be seen as a pun on Anne Hathaway's name in the penultimate line.

1 **love's** Venus's or Cupid's.
3 **languished for her sake** pined for her.
5 **Straight** immediately.
6 **ever sweet** always kind.

7 **Was used in giving** was accustomed to give.
  gentle doom generous judgement.

8 The woman taught her tongue to greet the poet in a different way.

9 **altered with an end** changed by adding an ending (see line 14).

10 **gentle day** foreshadows that the ending will be sweet.

11 The gentle day of the previous line is seen to contrast with night, which disappears like the fiend it is.

12 **is flown** fled.

13 The notion is that she threw the words away from the actual emotion.

14 The poet is saved from death by the addition of the words *not you* to *I hate* (line 13).

146

This is the only explicitly religious poem in the whole sequence.

1 **Poor soul** the poet directly addresses his soul.
  centre of my sinful earth the soul is at the centre of the body, as the earth is at the centre of the universe.

2 The soul has surrounded itself with material items (*rebel powers*), rather than looking to spiritual sustenance.

3 **pine** languish, starve.

4 Adorning the outward body with gaudy show, which is essentially meaningless.

5 **cost** expense.
  so short a lease a metaphor, imaging the human body as only briefly able to house the soul.

6 **fading mansion** continuing the metaphor, as the beautiful house is seen to fade quickly.

7 **inheritors of this excess** a reminder that the human body, after death, will be delivered into the waiting mouths of worms.

8 **charge** expense.
  Is this thy body's end? the poet asks if this is all the body was ever destined for.

9 **thy servant's loss** the loss of the body, which is servile to the soul.

10 The poet argues that it makes sense to allow the human body to languish (*pine*), in order that the soul can build up (*aggravate*) its store of plenty.

11 **terms divine** time that is heaven-sent and thereby permanent.
hours of dross wasted time, wherein useless material possessions are gathered.

12 **Within** inwardly.
without externally.

13–14 While Death feeds on the human body, the soul will remain victorious and feed on Death. See I Corinthians 15:26, 'The last enemy that shall be destroyed is death'.

147

1 **My love** the poet's obsession for his mistress.
fever love-sickness.

2 **nurseth the disease** prolongs his sickness.

3 **Feeding** gorging.

4 **uncertain sickly appetite** the faltering appetite of one who is ill.

5 **reason, the physician to my love** the rational mind of the poet, which attempts to argue with his irrational desire.

6 **prescriptions** the doctor's (reason's) prescribed remedy.

7 **desperate** in despair.
approve discover.

8 **Desire is death** desire can only lead to death.

9 Beyond caring, the poet acknowledges that he is beyond cure.

10 **frantic-mad** frantically mad.

11 **discourse** speech.

12 **At random from the truth** far from the truth.
vainly foolishly.

14 **as black as hell, as dark as night** both are proverbial and are used as comparisons for his mistress.

148

1 **What eyes** what kind of eyes.
love the emotion, or a more distinct force such as Cupid.

2 The poet's sense of sight seems not to correspond with what is truly there.

3 **if they have** if the poet's eyes really can see.
where is my judgement fled the poet contemplates that it may be his own distorted judgement that is the problem.

4 The blame would then fall upon the poet's distorted appraisal of what he sees.

5 A paradox, as the poet initially suggests that his mistress may well be fair, but then wonders if his eyes are false in their judgement of her.

6 **the world** popular opinion.

7 **If it be not** if it is not true that his mistress is fair.
love doth well denote my loving shows that.

8 **eye** vision, perhaps with a pun on 'ay' meaning 'yes'. The suggestion is that a doting eye can never be as truthful as the eyes of other, impartial, men.

9 **eye** vision, with a pun on 'I'.

10 **vexed** distressed.
watching and with tears the hallmark of unrequited love was said to be sleepless nights and weeping.

11 **No marvel** it is hardly surprising.

12 Even the sun cannot see until the sky is cleared of clouds.

13 **cunning** crafty.
love meaning the emotion, Cupid, and the mistress.

14 **eyes well-seeing** eyes that see the truth.

149

1 **O cruel** the mistress.

2 **partake** take sides.

3–4 The poet asks a rhetorical question, insisting that the mistress is always on his mind to the point that he forgets even about himself and his own best interests; indeed, he acts like a tyrant against himself for her sake.

5 The poet argues that anyone who hates his mistress is an enemy of his. See Psalm 139:21, 'Do I not hate them, O Lord, that hate thee?'.

6 **fawn upon** favour.
7 **lour'st** scowl.
  spend mete out, vent.
8 **present moan** current grief.
9 **respect** value.
10 **proud** splendid.
  thy service serving the mistress.
11 **all my best** all that is excellent in the poet.
12 **motion** a movement that suggests the poet should act.
13 The poet asks his mistress (*love*) to continue to treat him with contempt (*hate on*), because he now feels that he knows how her mind works.
14 The mistress only desires (*lov'st*) those men who recognize her true nature; because the poet has been blind to this, he is no challenge for her and is therefore an unworthy lover.

150

1 **from what power** the poet questions the power that gives his mistress strength.
2 **insufficiency** lack of worth.
  sway to command, to move.
3 **give the lie to my true sight** call my true vision a liar.
4 **brightness doth not grace the day** a metaphor connected to the idea that darkness is fair, if unconventionally so.
5 **becoming of things ill** the ability to make the ugly appear beautiful.
6 **refuse** worst, most worthless.
7 **warrantize** warranties.
8 **thy worst all best exceeds** a paradox, to suggest that the mistress's evils are better than the best of others.
10 **just cause of hate** a valid reason for hating.
11 **what others do abhor** that which others, who do not have a vested interest, have cause to despise.
12 **With others** along with others.
  abhor my state hate my emotional state, which is frenzied as a result of unrequited love.

13–14 Since the poet has found love in the mistress's unworthy traits, so she should love him and his; indeed, the very fact that he loves such a woman makes him even more worthy of her love.

151

1 **Love** Cupid.
2 **conscience** that which reminds us of what is right and wrong. The poet argues that conscience is actually born of love (sex).
3 **gentle cheater** an oxymoron (apparent contradiction in terms). **urge not my amiss** do not charge me with wrong.
4 Lest it transpires that the mistress is guilty of the poet's faults.
5 **thou betraying me** because the mistress betrays the poet.
6 **My nobler part** the soul. **my gross body's treason** the poet's body is treasonous because it overindulges in sex, thereby betraying its soul.
8 **flesh stays no further reason** the body waits for no other justification.
9 **rising** experiencing an erection.
10 **Proud of this pride** both (1) exulting in the triumphant prize and (2) proud of the erection.
11 **drudge** servant.
12 The word *stand* refers to the poet's erection, while *fall* suggests the penis's flaccid state after intercourse; it is also a war metaphor, suggesting that sex is like a military endeavour.
13 The poet argues that there is not an issue with his conscience.
14 The suggestion is that all that is remaining of their love is the physical act of sexual intercourse (the *rise and fall*).

152

1 **I am forsworn** the poet refers to an oath he has broken, perhaps to the youth.
2 **twice forsworn** the mistress is doubly perjured, as she has sworn her love to the poet.
3 **In act** the sexual act.

bed-vow broke   broken the marriage vow; the mistress has committed adultery.

new faith torn   new loving relationship abandoned. She has, metaphorically, also torn up her new contract of love.

4 **In vowing**   in professing.

new love bearing   experiencing a new affection. There may be a pun on 'bearing' another man's weight.

5–6 The poet insists that his own moral worth is even less than his mistress's.

7 **to misuse thee**   to treat the mistress badly, as well as to slander her.

8 The poet feels that integrity has been lost because of his faith in the mistress.

9 The poet states that he has only ever sworn that she is morally good.

11 **to enlighten thee**   to make the mistress seem more favourable.

gave eyes to blindness   by seeing both beauty and morals in a woman who has neither.

12 **swear against the thing they see**   make the eyes ignore the truth.

13 The poet now sees that his vision has lied to him in pronouncing his mistress to be fair. Note the pun on *eye* ('I').

14 **foul**   the notion is that it is a foul lie to insist that 'Fair is foul, and foul is fair' (*Macbeth* 1:1:11).

153

Sonnets 153 and 154 play on a conceit (extended metaphor) deriving from a six-line epigram by a sixth-century Byzantine scholar, Marianus Scholasticus. In both sonnets, the focus is Cupid and his 'brand' – a bawdy metaphor.

1 **laid by his brand**   put aside his flaming torch, *brand* being associated with Cupid and also carrying phallic connotations.

2 **a maid of Dian's**   a nymph or virgin of the goddess, Diana.

3 **steep**   quench.

4 **cold valley-fountain**   both (1) one of Diana's cool springs and (2) the vagina, which serves to cool the heat of the penis.

 5 **holy fire of love** Cupid's torch.
 6 **dateless lively heat** endless and desirous heat.
   still to endure to last forever.
 7 **grew** became.
   a seething bath boiling water.
   prove find out to be.
 8 **strange maladies** exotic diseases, which may also suggest venereal disease.
   sovereign potent.
 9 **new fired** newly ignited.
10 **for trial** to test (whether Cupid's torch is still aflame).
11 **withal** as a result (of being touched with Cupid's torch).
   help of bath desired wanted the restorative powers of a cool bath.
12 **hied** hurried.
   distempered diseased.
13 **for my help** for the poet's cure.
14 **my mistress' eyes** the poet's cure can only come from his mistress, whom he hopes will gaze upon him and weep with pity.

154

 1 **little Love-god** the young Cupid.
 2 Cupid's brand is to be seen as phallic.
 5 **fairest votary** the most beautiful virgin or nymph to Diana.
 6 **legions** multitudes.
 7 **general of hot desire** Cupid, as the commander of passion.
 8 **disarmed** left without a brand, or penis.
 9 **cool well by** cool spring nearby; with an allusion to the vagina (see Sonnet 153:4).
10 **love's** Cupid's.
11 **Growing** changing into.
   a bath a spring.
12 **thrall** prisoner.
13 **Came** with a pun on 'had an orgasm'.
14 Although hot springs can act as a curative, water can never cool down the heat of passion.

Interpretations

The sonnet sequence

The sonnet form is a particularly popular poetic construction in English verse and poets have written using this form for hundreds of years. The Shakespearean scheme, as we saw on page 14, was born of the original Italian form, with Shakespeare preferring the English rhyme scheme with its three quatrains and concluding couplet.

A body of 154 poems, written over an unspecified period of time, Shakespeare's sonnets have love as their central theme. They describe the love that a poet has for two different people: a young man and a dark lady. Comprised of two essential groups, Sonnets 1–126 are addressed to the youth, while 127–154 are to the woman. In these two sets of poems, a love triangle emerges whereby the woman, who was once the poet's mistress, has entered into a relationship with the youth. The youth and the poet have also been in a loving relationship – although its very nature is never made explicit – but this has ended due to unspecified reasons. The poet can only console himself with philosophical musings: if he has loved both the youth and the woman, and they have each loved him, then their new union makes all three of them as one.

Shakespeare's design

The question as to whether Shakespeare actually gave his approval for the sonnets to be published or for the enigmatic 'Mr W.H.' dedication has led to further queries, not least as to the 'correct' order in which the sequence should have been published. There are those who consider the publisher himself to have been instrumental in reordering the sonnets, therefore adding to the ambiguity of any narrative that might have come with them.

Critics have offered various groupings of the sonnets. C.F. Williamson (1976) argues that the sonnets are not sequenced randomly: the dark lady poems are separate from the youth poems; the first 17 have a common theme; there is a preoccupation with sleeplessness in Sonnets 27 and 28; the emotion of guilt is prevalent in Sonnets 33–5; the stolen mistress is the subject for 40–2; the image of the eye and the heart marks out 46–7; there is a journey in 50–1; the poet is preoccupied with death in 71–2; the Muse is invoked in 100–1; the 'Will' sonnets appear together at 135 and 136; and, from Sonnet 97 onwards, the poet is seen to be introspective. There is nothing here to be disputed and, depending upon interpretation, the reader can add still more valid groupings to the list. Sonnets 22–32 concern a love that is true; 33–42 are about a double betrayal; 43–52 indicate a melancholy in absence; 54–65 describe immortality; 66–77 present death and corruption; 78–86 concern themselves with the rival poet; 87–96 are about estrangement; while 97–108 present a love that has been revived and strengthened.

Activity

Discuss whether you think there is a specific design to Shakespeare's sonnet sequence.

Discussion

Just because some sonnets appear to be out of place to us, there could still be a sequence that we no longer recognize today. Shakespeare's sonnets do not present a story, as such: rather, they are a collection of little plots and there is no sense of conclusion at the close. Instead they tell of two people: a young man of high social ranking and great beauty (Sonnets 1–126) and a dark lady (Sonnets 127–52). The sequence opens with the poet advising the young man to marry and beget children (Sonnets 1–17), in order that his youthful beauty might be passed on. A rival poet begins to vie for the youth's affections (Sonnets 78–86), but the poet still promises to make the youth immortal through poetry. It is not clear when, but the poet has begun an affair with the lady, who is dark, both physically and metaphorically, and perhaps married to a man named William (Sonnets 135 and 136). It seems that the dark lady has had adulterous liaisons with men other than the poet and that the youth is her current conquest (Sonnets 133, 134 and 144).

Activity

According to Thomas P. Roche, 'Shakespeare's sequence is different from the majority of sequences in its almost unswerving allegiance to the pentameter fourteen-line form of the sonnet' (1989, p.79). However, there are three deviations. Name them and suggest why Shakespeare might have moved away from conventional patterns at these particular points in the sequence.

Discussion

- Sonnet 99: a poem made up of 15 lines, perhaps to indicate that there is an unlimited supply of flowers in the world, each of which has stolen its beauty from the youth.
- Sonnet 126: a poem of six couplets, which may well mark the end of the sequence on the youth. The number six is important, as it signals the perfection of the human, as well as the 'Beast of Revelation' (666) – the incarnation of evil described in the Bible. The number of the sonnet may also be significant with its 12 lines and six couplets, or as 63 multiplied by two. The number 63 was often associated with change and mortality, suggesting the imminent deaths of both the poet and the youth. The two pairs of empty brackets at the end of the sonnet may signal open graves, waiting to enclose their corpses.
- Sonnet 145: an octosyllabic poem, which some believe to be an early sonnet written while Shakespeare was wooing Anne Hathaway in about 1582.

The numbering of the sonnets

As you can see from the above discussion, numerical patterns do seem significant and provide some evidence that Shakespeare was writing his sonnet sequence in a very specific and logical order.

Activity

Identify and discuss any other examples where numbers are significant to the sonnet sequence.

Discussion

Here are a few ideas, cited by various critics over the centuries.

* Katherine Duncan-Jones suggests a reason why Sonnets 1–17 are so numbered: 'it may possibly relate to the fact that eighteen was the age at which young men were believed to be ready for consummated marriage' (1977, p.99).
* Sonnet 28 may well have been positioned in the sequence so as to tally with the length of the moon's monthly cycle, as well as the female menstrual cycle.
* The number 144 is the product of 12 times 12 and is often referred to as a 'gross'. Sonnet 144 describes the youth as fair, while the dark lady is demonic.
* Sonnet 52 has a reference to annual *feasts* (line 5) and the number 52 relates to the total number of weeks in the year.
* In the Early Modern period, to be 70 years of age was to be 'threescore and ten'. In contemporary thinking, this was considered to be the upper age limit for a human. It may be significant, then, that Sonnet 71 insists, *No longer mourn for me when I am dead* (line 1).
* The number 63 was associated with change and mortality, and Sonnet 63 is a poem where the poet imagines ageing and becoming senile. It is interesting that Sonnet 126 – which is the product of 63 times 2 – marks the completion of one of the cycle of sonnets.

Mr W.H.

The very compelling nature of the sonnets – where matters of desire, betrayal, and immorality mix – has led to many readers assuming that there must have been an autobiographical element to them. Despite more recent protestations arguing the contrary, it has proved too titillating to suppose that Shakespeare's life has engendered some of the sonnets' themes, ideas or characters for the idea to be left alone. Certainly, context must play some part and it is important to have a contextual background against which to set the sonnets. Therefore, since Shakespeare spent his working life in London, this will be our starting point.

In the sonnets, the description of the youth – even if not based on a particular London character – would certainly have been drawn from the London society of Shakespeare's day. Sonnet 25 compares the poet, who is an obscure but happy man of a low social class, with those men who enjoy a public life. The essential point is that such court favourites must always be on guard not to lose favour, since, *at a frown they in their glory die* (line 8). Shakespeare goes on to write of one such man:

> The painful warrior famoused for might:
> After a thousand victories, once foiled,
> Is from the book of honour razèd quite,
> And all the rest forgot for which he toiled   (9–12)

Over the years, interested readers have chosen the Earl of Southampton as one of the most fitting candidates here, since he was deprived of his title and imprisoned for his part in the 1601 Essex rebellion. Whether this is the case or not, many of the sonnets tell of the poet relishing the love that he and the youth share in the private sphere. Sonnet 107 has the poet describing his relationship as *fresh* (line 10) and this is matched by a very positive change in the public realm, which most probably corresponds with the successful accession of James I.

Activity
How might the youth be linked to the London royal court and its hierarchies? Use relevant sonnets to support your ideas.

Discussion
If the youth is to be seen as pure fiction, he is still a gentleman moving in high society. As well as celebrating his beauty and youth, the poet considers his high birth and far higher social status. In Shakespeare's

age, literary patronage was all and most scholars try to put a name to the 'Mr W.H.' of the dedication, hoping that he will provide the vital clue to the youth's identity. As we saw on pages 11–12, many theories have been put forward, some more tenuous than others:

- William Herbert, Third Earl of Pembroke (1580–1630), to whom Hemming and Condell dedicated the First Folio in 1623
- Henry Wriothesley, Earl of Southampton, to whom Shakespeare had dedicated *Venus and Adonis* (1593) and *The Rape of Lucrece* (1594)
- Anne Hathaway's brother, William Hathaway
- Anne Hathaway
- William Shakespeare, himself.

The last three suggestions are rather whimsical, based upon the notion of a Shakespeare who did not require literary patronage. Most academic scholars put some value in the first name since, according to reports, Pembroke was reluctant to marry and had a reputation for his generosity in the arts. His uncle was Philip Sidney and, as such, he had

A portrait of Henry Wriothesley, 3rd Earl of Southampton by an unknown painter

both the artistic and monetary background; and Shakespeare ought to have been happy with such a patron, even if such a hypothesis is unfounded.

W^m. HERBERT, EARL PEMBROKE.

Ob. 1630.

A portrait of William Herbert, 3rd Earl of Pembroke, painted by Daniel Mytens

However, the notion that the youth was a potential patron is somewhat flawed, since many of the sonnets see the poet rebuking the addressee. Sonnet 69 finds the youth's outer show to be flawless, while what lies beneath is foul and degraded; to the poet, the *rank smell of weeds* should be added to the *fair flower* (line 12) that is seen to the outward view. Sonnet 95 continues this theme, arguing that it is the young man's beauty that allows him freedom from criticism. Here, the youth is proverbially warned that, *The hardest knife ill-used doth lose his edge* (line 14), meaning that his promiscuity will lead to infertility. Sonnet 96 serves only as a mild rebuke, as the poet asks the youth to be faithful. He knows that this request is impossible, as the youth seems to be admired just as much for his faults as for his charms. He is given to wantonness and the poet both accuses and excuses him for this. In Sonnet 35, he calls himself an *accessary* (line 13) for making excuses for the youth, while Sonnets 40–2 have the poet desperately attempting to justify the youth's betrayal with his own mistress. Sonnet 89 even has the poet willing to take on the faults of which he is accused, promising to accept exclusion from the youth's company.

If we discount patronage as an option, then the search for the 'real' youth must begin with his unrivalled beauty. He is one of nature's *fairest creatures* (Sonnet 1:1), who shows himself to be *more lovely and more temperate* (Sonnet 18:2) than a summer's day. Indeed, such is his beauty that he rivals *A woman's face with nature's own hand painted* (Sonnet 20:1) and it is just this that *steals men's eyes and women's souls amazeth* (Sonnet 20:8). With a beautiful mind to match and the sort of upper-class lineage that demands the begetting of an heir, it becomes apparent that he is a nobleman with aristocratic tendencies.

As to the nature of the love that the poet feels for the youth, it might be well to remember Edmund Malone's remarks to his fellow editor, Steevens, on the issue of Sonnet 20:

> Such addresses to men, however delicate, were customary in our author's time and neither imparted criminality, nor were esteemed indecorous. To regulate our judgement of Shakespeare's poem by the modes of modern times, is surely as unreasonable as to try his plays by the rules of Aristotle.

In any case, this same sonnet refutes the idea that there is any semblance of a sexual relationship between the youth and the poet.

It should also be noted that Sonnets 127–54 have the dark lady as their central character, with the youth as the poet's rival for her affections.

Form, structure, and language

Predominantly a playwright, it was his poetry that brought Shakespeare the most literary success during his own lifetime. In just over a 20-year career, he wrote avidly and determinedly to produce a wealth of different poetic frameworks. His dramatic works are mostly composed of the rhythmic iambic pentameter, which plays with its stress pattern to determine certain effects. Variations on the basic iambic foot came in many ways. Sometimes, Shakespeare would add or subtract a syllable; he might invert the iamb and thus the stress pattern; or he might emphasize a rhythmic change by throwing in a caesural pause. More obvious alterations would come in the form of adding song lyrics to the script, a masque to aid performance, or by removing metric verse altogether, having characters speak in prose.

The metrical lessons learned from the plays can be seen in Shakespeare's non-dramatic verse. Every poem published was composed from iambic pentameter and Shakespeare can be seen to use the same techniques in his poetry as in his drama.

The sonnet

The sonnet is a lyric poem, consisting of one stanza made up of 14 lines. Each line is in iambic pentameter (ten syllables with the basic rhythm of an unstressed syllable followed by a stressed syllable). As we have seen, whereas the Italian sonnet was made up of an octave (eight lines, rhyming *abbaabba*) and a sestet (six lines of variant rhyme), Shakespeare's favoured form had three distinct quatrains (four lines, *abab cdcd efef*) and a final couplet (*gg*).

For Shakespeare, the theme or idea is developed through the quatrains, with the rhyme scheme marking off the three separate parts. At the beginning of each quatrain, there is a change of direction, no matter how slight, and the concluding comment is provided through the couplet.

Activity

Consider Sonnet 127. How does its metrical structure aid the presentation of meaning?

Discussion

This has a conventional structure, with the 14 lines being split into three quatrains and a final rhyming couplet. In terms of content:

- the opening quatrain deals with the issue of beauty, in a mock encomium. An encomium is a piece of writing held up in praise of someone or something. Since this rejoices in a dark complexion (the opposite of conventional contemporary beauty), it can be referred to as a paradoxical encomium
- the second quatrain suggests that beauty can no longer be held as sacrosanct, since falsely appropriated beauty is blasphemous. Alliteration on the letter 'f' (line 6) underscores the power of the theory of physiognomy, whereby the inner self ought to reflect the outer appearance
- the final quatrain opens with the word *Therefore* (line 9), which suggests that Shakespeare is about to draw a conclusion from his evidence. Indeed, he has the poet turn to rejoice in a mistress who is not conventionally beautiful, since she, at least, is naturally complexioned
- the rhyming couplet is introduced by the word *Yet* (line13), signalling the final refrain. The focus is upon the beauty of the mistress's dark eyes, which seem to mourn for other women who acquire their beauty artificially.

At the close of each quatrain is a change in tone, or direction, and this is known as the *volta*. Often, punctuation at the end of each quatrain serves to highlight such a change.

The numerous caesural pauses throw emphasis on the particularly significant: such as *profaned* (line 8); *not born fair* (line 11), which acts like a parenthetical point; and *mourn* (line 13). There is a change to the iambic rhythm in line 3; although there are the customary ten syllable beats, the stress falls upon the first syllable of *beauty*, perhaps highlighting the unconventional nature of *black* seeming beautiful.

Imagery

Shakespeare uses much imagery to signal his ideas, in particular metaphors and similes. Remember that a metaphor is a form of comparison that suggests *a* is *b*, rather than the simile which suggests that *a* is like *b*. There are shipping and legal metaphors in Sonnet 117, and Sonnet 97, for example, uses seasonal metaphors and similes to describe how the poet feels when the youth is away (*winter*) and when he is near (*summer*). While Sonnet 98 continues this imagery, Sonnet 99 uses a floral conceit (an extended metaphor) to depict the youth's beauty. Later in the collection, the poet compares his passion for the mistress to a disease, a conceit that paints him as a love-frenzied man devoid of all reason.

Activity

Edward Hubler wrote that Shakespeare, 'saw nature precisely and was always able to find the right words for her loveliness' (1952, p.30). Discuss some sonnets that demonstrate Shakespeare's use of nature imagery.

Discussion

Shakespeare can be seen to use natural imagery in his depictions of the various times of the day. For early morning, he uses many references to the plenitude of nature. For example, Sonnet 7 describes the sun as a *gracious light* (line 1), which *Lifts up his burning head* (line 2), while Sonnet 29 evokes the sense of sound with the *lark at break of day arising* (line 11). Sonnet 33 uses such natural imagery to depict the emotions of disappointment and betrayal better: *Full many a glorious morning have I seen* (line 1) before the sun must begin its afternoon descent, *permit*[ting] *the basest clouds to ride* (line 5), essentially obscuring the sun's blessings and *triumphant splendour* (line 10). Sonnets 27 and 28 have Shakespeare using day and night in opposition to show the claustrophobia that the poet feels in the darkness. The *swart-complexioned night* (Sonnet 28:11) draws out the poet's grief and only the imaginings of the youth make *black Night beauteous* (Sonnet 27:12).

The seasons also receive attention, as the poet initially demands that *winter's ragged hand* (Sonnet 6:1) be prevented from defacing the youth's *summer* (line 2). In order for this to happen, the youth must marry. When it becomes clear that the youth's fairness will not live on in his offspring, the poet insists that his own verse will immortalize his friend. In Sonnet 104, the poet notes,

> Three winters cold
> Have from the forests shook three summers' pride;
> Three beauteous springs to yellow autumn turned
> In process of the seasons have I seen; (lines 3–6)

It seems that the youth has looked in his mirror (Sonnet 103:6), only to see the signs of ageing. It is the poet's point that the youth will never age in his eyes nor in his sonnets, despite the nature metaphors which paint him as journeying from *fresh* (Sonnet 104:8) spring to a frozen winter. Other sonnets tell of *proud pied April (dressed in all his trim)* (Sonnet 98:2), along with *the lily's white* (line 9), the *forward violet* (Sonnet 99:1) and *the darling buds of May* (Sonnet 18:3). Sonnet 54 has at its centre the frequently cited rose; the *perfumed tincture* (line 6) that comes with its distillation into rose-water acts as a conceit to demonstrate the youth's everlasting beauty.

Activity

Much of Shakespeare's imagery is political, since the youth is implied to be a member of the aristocracy. Find some examples of imagery deriving from the world of politics or the public sphere.

Discussion

Living in London for the majority of his career, Shakespeare would have been well aware of political events, in terms of both national and international affairs. The battle with the Catholic Philip II of Spain, which culminated in the defeat of the Spanish Armada, left a deep impression upon the minds of the English. Shakespeare would have been no exception and some of the imagery used in his sonnets perhaps comes from such battles. For example, Sonnet 80 uses a shipping metaphor to contrast the poet with his rival. The poet is compared with a very small ship, often used by the English, as opposed to the rival's large Spanish galleon.

Activity

There are also many sonnets that describe the corruption and hypocrisy within the royal court. Two such examples are Sonnets 66 and 67. Analyse these two sonnets and the language used to show immoral behaviour.

Discussion

In Sonnet 66, we are given a catalogue of the chief morals that seem no longer to exist: *gilded honour* (line 5), *maiden virtue* (line 6), *right perfection* (line 7), *strength* (line 8), *art* (line 9), *skill* (line 10), *simple truth* (line 11) and *good* (line 12). As a result, the poet wishes not to live any longer, held back only by the love he has for his friend. The follow-on sonnet queries whether the youth ought to live in such a corrupt environment, being open to *infection* (line 1) and *impiety* (line 2). The poet's conclusion satisfies him: the youth ought to live as an example of what was once beautiful in a world that is now sinful and false.

Activity

Shakespeare often uses the language of the law and financial business in the imagery of his sonnets. Explore how Sonnet 87 uses such imagery to explain the relationship between the poet and the youth better.

Discussion

Essentially, the youth is *too dear* for the poet's purse. Being of a lowly status, the poet cannot afford his love. The vocabulary of this sonnet includes: *estimate* (line 2), *charter of thy worth* (line 3), *bonds* (line 4), *riches* (line 6), *gift* (line 7), *patent* (line 8), and *worth* (line 9), to name but a few. The poet feels that he has to relinquish his hold on the youth, since he is not deserving of him.

Analogies

If a simile is a comparison between two distinctly different things indicated by the words 'like' or 'as', then an analogy is an extended comparison. Sonnet 60 opens with an analogy, to show the speed of Time; *as the waves make towards the pebbled shore* (line 1), so every individual ages and decays. Sonnet 118 also uses an analogy, this time as a form of defence on the poet's part: he insists that any other relationships that he has entered into have been like eating unpalatable food or taking foul medicine to improve the appetite elsewhere.

Personification

Personification is an image related to metaphor, whereby an inanimate object or a concept is written as if it has human life. This provided a valuable tool for Shakespeare, especially when he alludes to ancient gods and goddesses and mythical figures. Examples come in the form of Cupid, Diana, Mars, Time, and Fortune. Can you list the sonnets that incorporate these figures?

Puns

A pun is a play on words, which are either identical in sound (homonym) or very similar in sound, but different in meaning. Shakespeare often puns on certain words for effect. The most famous of his puns is to be found in the 'Will' sonnets (135 and

136), where the word can mean 'inheritance contract', 'want', 'desire', 'penis' or 'William'. In a similar way, Sonnet 145 may pun on Anne Hathaway in line 13: *hate away.*

Metre

Shakespeare's metric line is iambic pentameter, but he often shifts the patterning in order to shape the poem's overall effect. For example, Sonnet 145 consists of octameters, a deliberate ploy to impose importance upon this poem.

The metre can also be altered through the use of pause. Shakespeare often uses the caesural pause, a strong pause which can provide emphasis or variety in a long pentameter line. Two other features are important in the metric movement of Shakespeare's sonnets and these can be identified very easily: (1) the natural, end-stopped pause that occurs at the end of a line; and (2) the run-on of the sense of the line with the use of enjambment. Look for examples of a caesura, an end-stopped line and enjambment, and try to determine why Shakespeare has used that particular device in each case.

Feminine endings are one method of shifting the regular rhythmical pattern. A feminine ending is the addition of one extra, unstressed syllable beat to a line of iambic pentameter. In Sonnet 33 Shakespeare uses this technique in the rhyming couplet, emphasizing that the youth is not like the *sun*, but is a mere son of the world. Sonnet 87 is the best example, where all the lines, except 2 and 4, have feminine endings. This may be to signal that this sonnet is a significant one in the sequence, since it marks the end of the rival poet section and the beginning of the downturn in the friendship between the poet and the youth.

Parallelisms

The first two lines of Sonnet 96 offer parallel ideas, designed to tell us a little more about the youth. One group considers *youth* and *wantonness* (line 1) to be his major fault, while another finds his *youth* and *gentle sport* (line 2) to be his major charm. It is interesting that *gentle sport* could allude to the youth's high social status. Sometimes, Shakespeare uses a parallelism in the same line, such as to mark the paradox of the youth's beauty in age: *As fast as thou shalt wane, so fast thou grow'st* (Sonnet 11:1).

Mode of address

For the most part, the poet directs his voice to a youth, a dark lady and a rival poet. However, dialogue is also established between the poet and the female Muse, a structural pattern peculiar to Renaissance verse. In this mode of address the poet sets up the fundamental epic question, the answer to which permeates the rest of the sonnet. In the case of Sonnets 100 and 101, Shakespeare has the poet blaming the Muse for allowing Time to ravage the beauty of the youth. She insists that the youth's beauty needs no adornment in poetry, but the poet argues to the contrary: he wants the Muse to aid him in his conquest to immortalize his beloved in poetry.

Hyperbole

Hyperbole is extravagant overstatement, used for either serious or comic effect. The poet spends much of his verse arguing that his language is plain and that he detests bold exaggeration for exaggeration's sake. He is insistent that other poets may idealize the youth, but that his own brand of understatement reflects his subtle and spiritual love for the young man. Nonetheless, hyperbole does abound as the poet describes his youth in hyperbolic conceits. Sonnet 112 is a prime example, whereby the poet explains that there is nothing in the world that matters to him except his friend. Other men may sully his reputation, but one positive word from the youth will remove all scandal and care.

Themes and ideas

Shakespeare's beliefs cannot be deduced from his poetry, but it is clear that he preoccupied himself with certain themes and ideas. Some of these are more prevalent than others. What follows is not an exhaustive list, but rather offers the dominant themes and ideologies that run throughout Shakespeare's sonnets.

Love

All of Shakespeare's sonnets are about love, whether it be the overwhelming happiness that comes with the feeling or the emotional outpouring of grief that is borne of its troubles and frustrations. The youth, the rival poet and the dark lady are unfaithful and immoral, causing the poet's failure to distinguish between true love and false. While this could reflect Shakespeare's experiences of love, there is no real evidence to support this. His marriage to Anne Hathaway lasted throughout his life and there are no reports about his having affairs with men or women. Shakespeare had three children and retired early so that he could return to his family in Stratford. Perhaps, then, Shakespeare's sonnets show either a conventional literary style of addressing love in all its forms, or – to satisfy those in need of an autobiographical element – an image of Shakespeare's view of what real love should not be.

Activity

To what extent is Sonnet 18 a poem about time as well as a love poem?

Discussion

This poem reinforces the notion that only *in eternal lines* (line 12) will the youth outdo death. Time is personified throughout the sequence as the figure who will catch up with the youth and the *summer's day* (line 1) comparison will be undermined. Shakespeare writes that *summer's lease hath all too short a date* (line 4), emphasizing the idea that this season has only a temporary tenancy on nature. It is the lines of poetry that will *give life* (line 14) to the youth in the absence of having children.

Absence

Twenty-three of the sonnets deal with the theme of absence, notably the idea that being apart from the youth will dissolve the friendship permanently. The established idea that the poet and the youth have become two souls in one body is also endangered and the poet begins to fear that his own sense of personal identity will be lost as a result.

Activity

In Sonnet 27, the poet describes himself as *Weary with toil* (line 1) and lacking in sleep, since his absence from the youth has led to sleeplessness. Find more examples of the theme of absence.

Discussion

There are many examples and only four more are offered here. Take these examples, and your own, and consider their meaning and overall significance.

> O absence, what a torment wouldst thou prove,
> Were it not thy sour leisure gave sweet leave
> To entertain the time with thoughts of love (Sonnet 39:9–11).

> All days are nights to see till I see thee,
> And nights bright days when dreams do show thee me
> (Sonnet 43:13–4).

> So either by thy picture or my love,
> Thyself away are present still with me (Sonnet 47:9-10).

> More flowers I noted, yet I none could see,
> But sweet or colour it had stol'n from thee (Sonnet 99:13-4).

Farewell sonnets

Sonnets 87–93 constitute what have become known as the 'farewell sonnets', in which the poet says goodbye to the youth for an unspecified reason.

Activity

Make a grid for these sonnets, charting the poet's farewell to the youth.

Discussion

Sonnet	Subject
Sonnet 87	The poet says his goodbye resignedly: *Farewell, thou art too dear for my possessing* (line 1).
Sonnet 88	The poet promises that he will shoulder all blame should the youth ever wish to renew their relationship: *... for thy right myself will bear all wrong* (line 14).
Sonnet 89	Following on from the last sonnet, the poet shows his willingness to accept all faults of which he is accused: *As I'll myself disgrace, knowing thy will* (line 7).
Sonnet 90	The poet urges the youth to reject him immediately, since he is already feeling very low: *Then hate me when thou wilt, if ever, now* (line 1).
Sonnet 91	The youth has it in his power to make the poet unhappy, since the latter values the youth's love more than any material possession: *Thy love is better than high birth to me, / Richer than wealth, prouder than garments' cost* (lines 9–10).
Sonnet 92	The poet hopes that once the youth has rejected him he will die: *... life no longer than thy love will stay* (line 3).
Sonnet 93	Despite being alone, the poet will be happy in his own self-deception, believing the youth always to have been faithful: *So shall I live, supposing thou art true* (line 1).

Anti-Petrarchan sonnets

The description of the dark lady differs remarkably from the conventional Petrarchan tradition, whereby the mistress is blonde, fair-complexioned and chaste. Shakespeare's dark lady is seen to radically subvert this tradition.

Activity

Which poems best define the dark lady as anti-Petrarchan?

Discussion

Sonnets 127 onwards have the dark lady as their focus and many of them mention her immorality and sexual wantonness. It is in Sonnet 127 that the poet states *now is black beauty's successive heir* (line 3) and that *every tongue says beauty should look so* (line 14). Sonnet 130 continues this anti-Petrarchan concept, describing the mistress as the antithesis of the hyperbolically praised conventional beauty. She has dark eyes, faded lips, dark-skinned breasts, black hair, and unperfumed breath. She certainly does not have rosy cheeks nor the tinkling voice that Petrarch's Laura has. Indeed, she is seen to walk, not as a goddess, but as a human, and it is this that shows other women to have been *belied with false compare* (line 14).

Not only is the dark lady physically different from Laura, she is also far from pure. Clearly, she is attainable and the poet's ardour has definitely been requited; and perhaps the only necessity is that the man should find the woman attractive. Any poetical physical description will probably misrepresent (*belie*) her in terms of deceiving similes (*false compare*). This leaves the youth to become the image of the unattainable – at least as far as the poet is concerned. It is the youth who is delineated as far superior to the mistress, and what we have before us is not a poet who finds himself in a conventionalized despair, but in a messy love triangle.

Religion

Shakespeare's background was of course Christian, but at no time in his sonnet sequence does he rely upon God or the concept of an after-life to redeem mortal ills. Occasionally, religion is replaced with mythology, such as in Sonnet 111, where the goddess Fortune is blamed for the poet's problems. Sonnet 146 is Shakespeare's only explicitly religious poem, where the poet addresses his soul, asking it why it relies upon gaudy show rather than spiritual riches. Man will triumph over death, only when the spirit triumphs over the physical.

Still more often, Shakespeare has the poet deifying the youth, such that he sacrilegiously places this new idol on a pedestal.

Activity

Does the poet present the youth as someone to be worshipped, in much the same way as one would worship God? Give examples of sonnets to explain your answer.

Discussion

Sonnet 105, *Let not my love be called idolatry* (line 1), is an example. Here, the poet associates the youth with the Holy Trinity, in that he worships him as *Fair, kind and true* (line 9), a phrase that is repeated several times over. The line, *To one, of one, still such, and ever so* (line 4) echoes the biblical, *such as the Father is, such is the Son: and such is the Holy Ghost*. This is a defining moment, ridding the sonnet form of its conventional master-mistress formula.

Ageing, death, and immortality

There is a real preoccupation with ageing and death in the poems. In the first 18 sonnets the poet urges the youth to marry and procreate so that his beauty can be passed on to future generations. The youth's lack of fidelity or commitment to one woman is hinted at and he is also accused of being a narcissist who will allow his physical assets to die with him. The poet can only hope to save the youth's idealized image in *pow'rful rhyme* (Sonnet 55:2), which will outlive *the gilded monuments / Of princes* (lines 1–2).

Activity

Consider Sonnets 1–18 and determine their success in attempting to convince the youth that he should beget children.

Discussion

The proposition is clear: that all natural beings are under an obligation to reproduce. The youth must be beautiful since the poet argues that from *fairest creatures we desire increase* (Sonnet 1:1), in order that *beauty's rose* (Sonnet 1:2) continues. As the Tudor emblem, the rose may well have reminded the reader that Queen Elizabeth I had no heir and that there was a definite urgency for her to marry and make certain England's future. Sonnet 8 insists that *Thou single wilt prove none* (line 14), arguing that without marriage there will be no harmony in the youth's life. At present, his unmatched beauty makes a *famine where abundance lies* (Sonnet 1:7), as he is seen to be guilty of hoarding his beauty.

Sonnet 2 warns the youth that there will come a time,

> When forty winters shall besiege thy brow,
> And dig deep trenches in thy beauty's field   (lines 1–2)

Only legitimate offspring will guard against the terrible prophecy, *Die single, and thine image dies with thee* (Sonnet 3:14). Sonnet 4, using a series of statements and questions, expands upon this argument, insisting that both God and Nature have endowed the youth with all of his charms and that it would be wrong to waste them. Sonnets 5 and 6 explain that, in the same way that roses can be distilled, the youth's essence can continue through procreation. Sonnets 9 and 10 have as their focus the premise that preserved beauty – that which is *kept unused* – will be so *destroy*[ed] (Sonnet 9:12) in the process.

Sonnets 12, 15, and 16 introduce Time, personified, who will make it his business to age and then destroy the youth. It is *this bloody tyrant* (Sonnet 16:2) upon whom the youth should *Make war* (line 2), and only children can defy the unstoppable advance of time:

And nothing 'gainst Time's scythe can make defence
Save breed to brave him when he takes thee hence.

(Sonnet 12:13–14).

However, the poet's various frameworks of much the same advice work to convince us of the youth's disinclination toward marriage. The reader is reminded of the opening sonnet, where the youth was described as being *contracted to thine own bright eyes* (line 5). Essentially, the youth's eyes are narcissistic in their love, turning ever inward; and, as a consequence, his beauty will go to waste, ultimately going to the grave.

Activity

While Shakespeare's early sonnets to the youth deal with the urgency for procreation, the later sonnets are very much bound up with ideas of death and decay. How might Sonnet 126 be seen as a fitting completion of the 'fair youth' sequence?

Discussion

Sonnet 126 is often termed a non-sonnet, since it is structured in six-couplet form, with only 12 lines in total. The *lovely boy* (line 1) is probably the youth, who has been lent to the poet by Nature. Even she must ultimately return him to the hands of Time and then to death. There is a definite *volta* at the end of the eighth line, powered by a full stop, with the emphasis thrown upon the verb *kill*. The final two couplets are introduced by the word *Yet* to mark the final refrain, and the exclamation of line 10 signals a very certain conclusion. Although lines 11 and 12 make perfect sense in themselves, there is the sense that the poem is unfinished. The gaping parentheses that ensue only serve to further stress that silence. Over the years, critics have viewed the parentheses in various ways: as the shape of an empty hourglass, as the moon and its changing shape, and as a reference to the grave. Ultimately, they signal that something should be there, but is not: and so the youth's life is incomplete.

Time

The image of Time as a personified character, cloaked in black and carrying a scythe, was a common one during the Early Modern period. In Renaissance drama, he was often depicted as a character called Mower, a metaphor also closely allied with the notion of cutting down freshly grown grass or hay. The poet directly addresses Time on many occasions, mostly in anticipation of the death of his friend. Sonnet 64 surveys Time in such a way, being formally organized into three distinct quatrains, each opening with the phrase *When I have seen*. The preposition *when* indicates the ruination that Time will wreak in the future. The poet's response to what he will see comes in the couplet, as he imagines a definitive death, which causes sorrow even in expectation.

Activity

Identify some more important references to time in the sonnets.

Discussion

Consider as many possible uses of the concept as you can. Here are a few examples to get you started.

Sonnet	Reference	Significance
2	*forty winters* (line 1)	part of a conceit, stressing the destructive hand of time
22	*time's furrows* (line 3)	a metaphor, using fertility imagery to present time
49	*Against that time* (line 1)	this phrase is repeated throughout the sonnet, as the poet anticipates a time when the youth no longer cares for him
65	*swift foot* (line 11)	Time is personified as a speedy sprinter
116	*Love's not Time's fool* (line 9)	Time has power over everything except love

From these examples, it is clear that Shakespeare's allusions to Time tend to come in the earlier sonnets, when he addresses the youth. Firstly, because the poet sees the sense in his friend marrying and procreating to preserve his own image and, secondly, because immortality is seen to come with art.

Morality

Many sonnets deal with the hypocrisy and deceit of the royal court life that Shakespeare would have become familiar with. The men who are attracted to the youth are described as being ambitious courtiers who aspire to greater things. These are the very individuals who ought not to be raised to power, since their methods are unethical. What comes as a great disappointment to the poet is his discovery that the youth's outer beauty is not a true reflection of his inner soul.

Activity

Explore any one, or more, sonnet(s) that deal(s) with the theory of physiognomy.

Discussion

There are many possible sonnets to choose from since this is an important concept in Petrarchism. Sonnets 92–5 deal with physiognomy, as the poet acknowledges that the youth *mayst be false, and yet I know it not* (Sonnet 92:14). In Sonnet 93 the ninth line opens with the conjunction *But*, turning the mood from an acceptance of being *Like a deceivèd husband* (line 2) to the notion of how disastrous such a deception can actually prove to be:

> How like Eve's apple doth thy beauty grow,
> If thy sweet virtue answer not thy show   (13–14)

The final line of Sonnet 94 uses a floral metaphor to drive home the point: because virtue is expected in the beautiful, the lack of virtue seems so much the worse. Sonnet 95 concludes this set by suggesting that the immoral youth has been given excessive freedom as a result of his outer sweetness and loveliness. The poet exclaims at the *mansion* (line 9) that the vices are housed in and how this may well affect the youth adversely in the end. The final line refers to such a *privilege* (line 13) in terms of an image – *The hardest knife ill-used doth lose his edge* (line 14) – and this probably refers to the youth's promiscuity threatening his sexual potency or attractiveness.

Critical views

Unlike the reception of Shakespeare's early narrative poems, which were received with great applause, the 1609 quarto sonnet sequence was met with a relative lack of enthusiasm.

The very young Metaphysical poet, George Herbert, wrote to his mother at the end of 1609, disappointed with Shakespeare's poetic output of that year. He referred in two poems of his own to current 'Sonnets', which did not incorporate religious devotion, but only secular idolatry. This was hardly the sort of response that a, by that time, famous William Shakespeare would have wanted for his sonnet sequence. Indeed, the very few devotees of his sonnet material were to make only passing reference to it.

The 1640 edition of the sonnets seemed to carry a little more literary weight, not least because John Benson reorganized the sequence. With help from other experienced editors, he reordered and merged the poems, adding lines to minimize or negate any meanings that he considered to be offensive or ambiguous. Unfortunately, this served only to decrease the sonnets' popularity with the general readership.

In the eighteenth century, Samuel Johnson's edition of Shakespeare included a *Supplement* by Edmund Malone, who criticized the sonnet form as a genre and labelled Shakespeare's own attempts as perplexing. In 1793, George Steevens published his edition of Shakespeare's plays, decrying the sonnets as having been deliberately excluded, 'because the strongest act of

Parliament that could be framed, would fail to compel readers into their service' (Rollins, Vol. 2, p. 337). Succeeding decades served only to compound the sonnets' lack of success, not least because they were considered confusing and as enigmatic as the writer himself.

However, by 1827, the well-thought-of Romantic poet, William Wordsworth, went to the opposite extreme and asked critics to 'Scorn not the Sonnet', especially those of Shakespeare, as they represented the 'key [with which he] unlocked his heart'. Samuel Taylor Coleridge also appreciated the sequence, although he struggled somewhat with its sexual element. In 1833, he tried to reconcile this issue with himself by deciding that Shakespeare's passionate nature could only have been borne from the love of a woman, not the love of a man.

Despite denying his interest in the sonnets, the Poet Laureate, Alfred Lord Tennyson, was fascinated by Shakespeare's work, using it as a model for his *In Memoriam* (1850). In the second half of the same century, Oscar Wilde directly praised the sonnets, expressing that he 'loved them, as one should love all things, not wisely but too well' (1899, *Letters*, number 789).

By the twentieth century, J.W. Mackail (*Approach to Shakespeare*, 1930, p. 118) argued that Shakespeare's sonnets ought to be studied as poems for their own sake. The New Criticism theory of the 1930s helped to drive this belief, which insisted upon close reading and not contextualization. Rejecting any autobiographical implications, Mackail placed Shakespeare above all other great sonneteers: 'But just as Shakespeare's dramatic work eclipses that of his contemporaries [...] so beside Shakespeare's sonnets the whole mass of other Elizabethan sonnet-literature pales and thins'. In the same year, Thomas Seccombe and J.W. Allen found the sonnet sequence to be one of 'the most splendid legacies left by Elizabethan England'. They considered the decision to direct many of his poems to a man to be 'remarkable' and, along with the idea of addressing sonnets to a dark lady, it only demonstrated Shakespeare's originality in a world of convention (*The Age of Shakespeare*, 1903, Vol. I).

In 1934, L.C. Knights wrote of Shakespeare being fascinated by two major themes – man's personality and how Time alters it. It was Knights's view that such themes were what preoccupied Shakespeare, rather than a decision to present his own life in verse ('Shakespeare's Sonnets', *Scrutiny*, III, p. 152). Thomas Marc Parrott felt much the same, considering the themes of Beauty and Time to be paramount, driving the narrative in a way that autobiography never could. It was also Parrott's belief that some of the sonnets are better than others and that each should be judged on its own merit (*William Shakespeare*, 1934, p. 193).

In his 1964 edition, W.H. Auden wrote that 'more nonsense has been talked and written, more intellectual and emotional energy expended in vain, on the sonnets of Shakespeare than on any other literary work in the world' (*The Sonnets*, Signet Classics, 1964, p. xvii). He was one of the first editors to write of how the Shakespearean sonnet form – with its three quatrains and concluding couplet – complemented the content of his sonnets and the development of each one of his rhetorical arguments. For Auden, it was the language, style, and structure that was of the utmost importance, and any mythmaking only served to criticize unfairly the sonnet sequence as a whole.

C.S. Lewis was another great admirer of the sonnets, arguing that the most gratification comes from refusing to read the sequence like a novel: since 'the precise mode of love which the poet declares for the man remains obscure' (*English Literature in the Sixteenth Century*, 1954, pp. 498–509). His view was that the sonnets do not fit a neat narrative structure and are not meant to do so. Essentially, 'the emotion expressed by the sonnets refuses to fit into any pigeon-holes'.

It was the post-war critic, Stephen Booth, who refused to allow the autobiographical debate to blind his vision. When reading other commentators' attempts to pin down Shakespeare's sexuality, for example, Booth dismissed the whole concept as ludicrous; for him 'William Shakespeare was almost certainly homosexual, bisexual or heterosexual. The sonnets provide no evidence on the matter' (1977, p. 548). Such a perception was to continue amongst other open-minded individuals for years. John Kerrigan was to argue that the relationship between the poet and the youth is one of 'comradely affection' (p. 55) and nothing more, viewing many of the other theories to be intolerable and 'crackpot' (1986, p. 74).

More recent scholars, of the late twentieth and early twenty-first centuries, have opened their minds still further to a wide variety of possible meanings behind the sonnets, some of them rarely, or never, touched upon before. In addition, the twentieth century welcomed female editors and commentators to share their views on Shakespeare's sonnets, in a predominantly male-oriented critical field. Now it is customary to judge the sonnets not necessarily as a whole sequence, but considering each 'little poem' in its own right. It is acknowledged that critics do not know everything about sixteenth-century poetic conventions and there may well have been patterns – some of which Shakespeare followed – that we are not familiar with.

In most recent years there has been an influx of the sort of criticism that is open to any possibility. It has become important to note that each individual sonnet performs its own narrative, perhaps blending with short narrative structures within the whole sequence. It has become acceptable – and intelligent – to see Sonnets 1–154 as a quasi-narrative (apparent but not real), this having been the Early Modern convention and what makes the sonnet sequence more interesting by modern standards.

Essay Questions

Worked questions

The two questions below are followed by some points you might address in your response.

1 **Do you consider Shakespeare's sonnet sequence to have been placed in the correct chronological order? Choose examples to explore whether the chronology matters.**

As long as your chosen sonnets are relevant, it is up to you which you focus on. Once you have made that decision, you need to decide on the framework for your argument. A plan is always advisable. Here are a few ideas to get you started:

- The order of Shakespeare's sonnet sequence has been one of its main sources of contention, with many editors and critics suggesting a reordering. In 1640, the publisher, John Benson, completely rearranged the 1609 quarto edition. As well as placing them into what he considered to be a more comprehensible sequence, he also placed as many as five sonnets together to make longer poems. Each new poem was given a title, which Benson clearly thought would make the sequence more like a story.
- The order in which Thorpe had presented the 1609 quarto edition ran as follows: a) Sonnets 1–17, asking the youth to marry, bear children and preserve his fairness; b) 18–126, addressed to the male youth; c) 127–152, addressed to the dark lady; and d) two conventional love sonnets on Cupid. However, it is the doubt concerning Shakespeare's involvement in the publication of the 1609 edition that has led to the question as to the validity of the chronology.
- In the 1780 edition, the editors, Malone and Steevens, used Thorpe's order but voiced some dissatisfaction with it. For

them, there was no logic to the dark lady sequence and its addition served only to mar the continuity of any semblance of a story that preceded it. Ensuing critics, with this same belief, were to consider Sonnets 40–2 – where the youth is accused of, and forgiven for, stealing the poet's mistress – to be about the dark lady, thus further disproving the completeness of the cycle of 1–126.

- There remain many critics who insist that there is no linguistic or literary evidence to support the argument that Sonnets 1–126 are each addressed to a young man. Moreover, there is no evidence to suggest a homosexual relationship between the pair, especially in the light of Sonnet 20, where the poet refutes such a notion. As a result, do Sonnets 1–126 need to be together, or even in the 1609 order?

- The addition of the rival poet could well mean that it is the love affair with the mistress that is all-important and not any sort of affair with the youth. Should Sonnets 127–52, then, be prioritized chronologically?

- There are those who are dissatisfied with the last two sonnets as a conclusion to the sequence since they do not seem to serve as a conclusion.

- It is important to note the conventions of sonnet writing in that the sonnet sequence was never a way of telling a complete story. Since there are narrative elements contained within Shakespeare's sequence, it might be better to describe it as a quasi-, or apparent, narrative. Clearly, the question of autobiography – and the efforts to discover who might fit the roles of the characters – has added to the drive to shape the sequence into a story that can tell us more about Shakespeare, the man.

2 Shakespeare's verse looks at an idealised romantic picture that is firmly rooted in the considerations of Petrarchism. Do you agree?

With a question like this, it is necessary for you to provide a definition of 'Petrarchism' as a frame of reference for your choice of poems. The main points to remember about Petrarchism are:

- There is not one overriding definition of the term, but it began with the thirteenth-century Italian poet, Francesco Petrarca.
- The term 'Petrarchism' was coined well after Petrarch was dead, as the main traits of his own style of poetry continued and developed.
- It is a literary school firmly rooted in its historical context. It may also be relevant to mention the convention of courtly love and those English sonneteers that brought Petrarch's sonnet style to England.
- Of the traits that Petrarchist sonneteers had in common, the most important rested with the fair-complexioned woman, who was pursued and idealized by the Italian courtier. It is important to note that the courtier's love would never be requited. Shakespeare does tap into this style in order to both emulate and subvert it most notably in Sonnet 130, where the poet boasts of his mistress's lack of conventional beauty. Again, in Sonnet 132 he praises the dark beauty of his lady love, determining:

> Then will I swear beauty herself is black,
> And all they foul that thy complexion lack. (13–14)

In his description of the youth, the poet similarly subverts the Petrarchan tradition – but we should remember that it was conventional to praise men as well as women, using the blazon, an idealistic form of praise.

Sample questions

The following questions are for you to try.

1   What evidence can you present to support the view that Shakespeare's sonnets are autobiographical?

2   In what ways and in which sonnets does Shakespeare indicate that time can be conquered?

3   What do you consider to be the dominant themes in Shakespeare's sonnet sequence? Use examples to illustrate.

4   How far would you argue that the context of the period in which Shakespeare wrote is vital to the completed sonnets?

5   Do you consider Shakespeare to have been revolutionary in addressing the majority of his sonnets to a young man? Choose relevant poems to substantiate your argument.

6   Why do you think that Shakespeare deviates so seldom from the conventional sonnet form in his sequence? Give examples of where he does so and discuss the effects achieved.

7   One of the many interesting elements in Shakespeare's sonnets is his use of nature imagery. Explore, with use of examples.

8   Shakespeare makes a plea for honesty in his sonnets, insisting that he writes 'rude lines' without fanciful metaphors, affected language or extravagant exaggeration. Is this plea correct? Choose poems to best exemplify you answer.

Chronology

Events in Shakespeare's life

1564	Born in Stratford-upon-Avon.
1582	Marries Anne Hathaway.
1583	Daughter, Susanna is born.
1585	Twins, Hamnet and Judith, born.
1585–92	At some point in this period, moves to London.
Late 1580s to early 1590s	Begins to write his first plays for performance.

Historical events

1534	Henry VIII breaks with Rome.
1558	Elizabeth I accedes to throne. Thomas Kyd born.
1564	Christopher Marlowe born.
1568	Mary Queen of Scots imprisoned by Elizabeth I.
1572	John Donne and Ben Jonson born.
1576	Erection of London theatres – the Theatre and the Curtain.
1577	Francis Drake sets out on round the world voyage. Raphael Holinshed's *Chronicles of England, Scotland and Ireland* are published
1582	Plague outbreak in London.
1587	Execution of Mary Queen of Scots, after implicated in plot to murder Elizabeth I. First performance of Marlowe's *Tamburlaine the Great*.
1588	The Spanish Armada defeated.

Events in Shakespeare's life

1593	*Venus and Adonis* published.
1594	*The Rape of Lucrece* published. Writes exclusively for the Lord Chamberlain's Men.
1596	Granted coat of arms. Hamnet dies.
1597	Buys New Place.
1599	Globe Theatre opens. Shakespeare buys a share in it. Poetry anthology *The Passionate Pilgrim* is published, containing versions of two of his sonnets (138 and 144).
1603	Lord Chamberlain's Men come under the patronage of James I, to become the King's Men.
1609	Becomes part-owner of the indoor playhouse, the Blackfriars Theatre. The complete *Sonnets* are published.
1613	The Globe burns down.
1614	Second Globe opens.
1616	Dies 23 April.

Historical events

1589	Kyd's *The Spansh Tragedy* and Marlowe's *The Jew of Malta* probably first performed.
1592	Plague in London. Playhouses closed.
1594	The playhouses re-open.
1596	Drake dies on expedition to West Indies.
1598	Marlowe publishes his narrative poem, *Hero and Leander*.
1603	Death of Queen Elizabeth I. Accession of James I. Plague causes playhouses to close.
1605	Guy Fawkes's plot to blow up the Houses of Parliament.

Further Reading

Primary sources

John Benson (publisher), *Poems Written by Wil. Shakespeare. Gent.* (London, 1640); also available in facsimile, H.M. Klein (ed.) (Hildesheim, 1979)

G. Blakemore Evans (ed.), *Shakespeare's Sonnets: Undated Edition* (Cambridge University Press, 2006)

Stephen Booth, *Shakespeare's Sonnets: Edited with Analytic Commentary* (London, 1977)

Katherine Duncan-Jones (ed.), *Shakespeare's Sonnets* (Arden Shakespeare, 1997)

G.B. Evans, (ed.), *Shakespeare's Sonnets* (Cambridge University Press, 1996)

John Kerrigan (ed.), *The Sonnets and A Lover's Complaint* (New Penguin Books, 1986)

Edmond Malone (ed.), *Supplement to the Edition of Shakespeare's Plays*, published in 1778: *Poems*, Vol 1. (London, 1780), pp. 397–760

Frances Meres, *Palladis Tamia: Wit's Treasury* (1598; D.C. Allen, 1933)

Hyder E. Rollins (ed.), *The Poems* (New Variorum Shakespeare, 1938)

Martin Seymour-Smith (ed.), *Shakespeare's Sonnets*, (Heinemann, 1963)

Stanley Wells (ed.), *The Sonnets* (Oxford University Press, 1985)

Secondary sources

M.H. Abrams, *A Glossary of Literary Terms* (Holt, Rinehart and Winston, 1988)

Alan Bray, *Homosexuality in Renaissance England* (Gay Men's Press, 1982)

Margreta de Grazia and Stanley Wells (eds.), *The Cambridge Companion to Shakespeare* (Cambridge University Press, 2001)

Robert M. Durling (ed. and trans.), *Petrarch's Lyric Poems: The 'Rime sparse' and Other Lyrics* (Harvard University Press, 1976)

Robert Ellrodt, 'Shakespeare the Non-Dramatic Poet', in *The Cambridge Companion to Shakespeare Studies*, ed. by Stanley Wells (Cambridge University Press, 1986)

Leonard Forster, *The Icy Fire: Five Studies in European Petrarchism* (Cambridge University Press, 1969)

Robert Giroux, *The Book Known as Q: A Consideration of Shakespeare's Sonnets* (Weidenfeld and Nicholson, 1982)

Jonathan Goldberg (ed.), *Queering the Renaissance* (Duke University Press, 1984)

Andrew Gurr, *Playgoing in Shakespeare's London* (Cambridge University Press, 1987)

Michael Hattaway (ed.), *A Cambridge Companion to English Renaissance Literature and Culture* (Blackwell Publishers, 2000)

Alan Haynes, *Sex in Elizabethan England* (Sutton Publishing, 1997)

Graham Holderness (ed.), *The Shakespeare Myth* (Manchester University Press, 1988)

Leslie Hotson, *Shakespeare's Sonnets Dated, and Other Essays* (Hart-Davis, 1964)

Edward Hubler, *The Sense of Shakespeare's Sonnets* (Princeton University Press, 1952)

Kenneth Muir, *Shakespeare's Sonnets* (Allen and Unwin, 1979)

David Norbrook, *Poetry and Politics in the English Renaissance* (Routledge and Kegan Paul, 1976)

Christopher Ricks (ed.), *New History of Literature, II: English Poetry and Prose, 1540–1674* (Barrie and Jenkins, 1970)

Thomas P. Roche, *Petrarch and the English Sonnet Sequence* (AMS Press, 1989)

A.L. Rowse, *Shakespeare's Sonnets: The Problems Solved* (Macmillan, 1973)

A.L. Rowse, *Shakespeare's Southampton* (Macmillan, 1965)

Gamini Salgado, *The Elizabethan Underworld* (Sutton Publishing, 1992)

Bruce R. Smith, *Homosexual Desire in Shakespeare's England: A Cultural Poetics* (University of Chicago Press, 1991)

Brents Stirling, *The Shakespeare Sonnet Order* (University of California Press, 1968)

Lawrence Stone, *The Family, Sex and Marriage in England, 1500–1800* (Weidenfeld and Nicholson, 1977)

M.P. Tilley, *A Dictionary of the Proverbs in England in the Sixteenth and Seventeenth Centuries* (University of Michigan, 1950)

E.M. Tillyard, *The Elizabethan World Picture* (Penguin, 1990)

Helen Vendler, *The Art of Shakespeare's Sonnets* (Belknap Press of Harvard University Press, 1999)

David K. Weiser, *Mind in Character: Shakespeare's Speaker in the Sonnets* (University of Missouri Press, 1987)

Stanley Wells (ed.), *Shakespeare: A Bibliographical Guide* (Oxford University Press, 1990)

C.F. Williamson, 'Themes and Patterns in Shakespeare's Sonnets', *Essays in Criticism* 26 (1976)

F.P. Wilson, *The Plague in Shakespeare's London* (Oxford University Press, 1927)